Letters from a former Dean

Advice for students on navigating their studies to a successful career

Emeritus Professor Trevor Heath

OAM, BVSc (Syd), MA(Ed) (Mich State), MHPEd (NSW),
PhD (ANU), DVSc (Qld) DVSc honoris causa (Syd), FACVSc

AUSTRALIANACADEMICPRESS

First published 2021 by:
Australian Academic Press Group Pty. Ltd.
Samford Valley QLD, Australia
www.australianacademicpress.com.au

A catalogue record for this
book is available from the
National Library of Australia

Letters from a former Dean: Advice for students on navigating their studies to a successful career
ISBN 9781925644463   (paperback)
ISBN 9781925644470   (ebook)

Disclaimer
Every effort has been made in preparing this work to provide information based on accepted standards and practice at the time of publication. The publisher and author, however, make no representations or warranties with respect to the accuracy or completeness of the contents of this book and specifically disclaim any implied warranties of merchantability or fitness for a particular purpose. It is sold on the understanding that the publisher is not engaged in rendering professional services and neither the publisher nor the author shall be liable for damages arising herefrom. If professional advice or other expert assistance is required, the services of a competent professional should be sought.

Publisher & Editor: Stephen May

Cover design: Luke Harris, Working Type Studio

Cover photos: Trevor Heath

Typesetting: Australian Academic Press

Printing: Lightning Source

Education is the acquisition of the art of the utilisation of knowledge.

Alfred North Whitehead, (1861–1947)
English mathematician and philosopher

It is incredibly rewarding to be able to provide a foreword to this collection of wisdom from a lifetime of service in tertiary education.

I first met Trevor when I was a 17-year-old high school student, and Trevor was the incumbent Dean of Veterinary Science at The University of Queensland (UQ). I was considering veterinary science as a career option and sought advice on the program, future career prospects and the pros and cons of deferring for a year before commencing study. I joined UQ as a BVSc student a little over a year later.

During my time at UQ Trevor was a competitor in squash and a mentor at other times, even an occasional classroom teacher. As I write this foreword it is 40 years since I entered first year BVSc.

Trevor's advice to me as a young student in a rapidly changing world was supportive, understanding and non-judgemental. It was delivered in a clear and friendly manner along with an obvious depth of experience, knowledge and empathy.

Even today, I can clearly recall specific conversations with Trevor that have resonated with me over the years and that have guided my decisions at key points in my own career.

This book provides a series of short letters, written by a sage, harvested from a lifetime of direct interactions with real people, and flavoured by a deep scientific curiosity and understanding of the human condition. The topics cover the full range of issues that almost all of us have encountered (or will) in our lives. Each letter is short, easily digestible, thought provoking and insightful.

These letters remind me of conversations I have had with Trevor over four decades but most particularly those I enjoyed when I was a BVSc student.

Thank you Trevor for your devotion to teaching, supporting and mentoring. You have had (and continue to have) a direct and meaningful impact on a vast number of individuals across multiple generations. We are better off as a result of those interactions.

I commend this book to students of today — and tomorrow.

Professor Nigel Perkins
BVSc (UQ), MS (Ohio State), PhD (Massey), FANZCVSc
Head of School and Dean, School of Veterinary Science, The University of Queensland

Contents

Section 4 **Looking Forward**

Section 5 **Distilling the Essence**

An Explanation

I hope that you will find these tips helpful as you make the transition to higher study, then navigate through your course and enter the workforce. Or if you are already at some point along that continuum.

They are based on more than 60 years as a student, teacher, supervisor, mentor, research worker, and/or administrator at six universities in Australia and two in the USA. Although my career involved stints in managerial roles including Dean and Head, my passion remained to help students — through teaching, supporting and mentoring — to achieve their objectives in their studies, profession and life generally.

That passion led to the idea of passing on what I have learned, and this is the result. From the beginning, I have done that in a series of letters to the reader. I hope that you will find that form comfortable, even if more used to receiving messages in other forms.

Although some of the letters are a bit prescriptive, most are intended to provide grist for the cerebral mill; to provide a basis for reflection rather than instructions to be followed.

For the most part, I have written about things I have learned from my students, both while they were at university and after they graduated.

I am hugely indebted to all of them, as I have learned far more from them than they could imagine. But I have also been keen to understand the relevant underlying principles, and to that end undertook masters degrees in educational psychology and medical education, and in health personnel education, and published more than 60 papers in these fields (sorry about the self-promotion, but felt I should give a bit of background).

One principle that has guided these interactions with young people is the knowledge that a small amount of help at a critical point in their life can have an effect out of proportion to the time and effort involved. My objective has always been to encourage them to work towards a solution, to develop the wit and the will to solve problems for themselves. I have gained enormous pleasure and satisfaction from doing this, and am hugely grateful for being allowed into the lives of so many young people.

The letters are arranged in a time-based sequence, starting with entering university and ending in the workplace and beyond, although there are some detours relevant to life in general. You may notice that I have revisited some points in different letters. This partial duplication is deliberate as I believe that they are important in the context of each letter. This also makes it possible to dip into the series at any point, without having read previous letters.

I do not claim any special expertise; my objective is to provide a basis for reflecting on relevant issues in the hope of reaching an outcome that works for each person. I hope that you find them of some value and that you have a satisfying, productive, rewarding, happy and healthy career and life generally.

Becoming A Successful Student

The first letter...

Congratulations on being accepted into university. I wish you all the best of good luck and good fortune as you navigate the opportunities that come your way, and set yourself up for a rewarding, successful and happiness-inducing career and life generally.

I thought it might be helpful if I passed on some thoughts from a lifetime of working with young people entering university. I have set them out as a series of letters, covering the period from the start of university studies to postgraduate life and career.

The first series deals with life as a student, and I encourage you to look to the future and to take advantage of opportunities to develop skills and other aptitudes that will be useful later. Many students see their student years only to gain a degree, but they can be much more.

Through sporting, social, cultural, professional and community activities, it is possible to develop contacts that may be useful later, as well as practical skills and ways of thinking about work and life generally that can be of immense value in the future. Of course, it is essential to maintain an effective balance between the course-related and other activities and to keep in mind that, valuable though the other activities are, studies must be the major focus.

The next series addresses issues related to the health of heads, of believing in yourself and of interacting in a sensitive and effective way with other people, including those near and dear.

These are followed by some focused on preparing for, seeking, and getting, a position that will match your passion and abilities, and some intended to help prepare yourself for the technological changes that will change workplaces and lives generally.

I hope that they will not seem too much like sermonising for my objective is to provide a basis for thinking about how to approach the various issues that you will confront over the years ahead.

I do not claim to be a font of all wisdom; rather a concerned colleague and friend who has tried to unravel issues brought by the many young people who have been generous enough to let me into their lives.

I hope you will find them helpful, and that you will let me know whenever you feel that I may be able to help you in other ways.

I offer my very best wishes for a successful, satisfying, enjoyable — and healthy — time at university, and later in your working and personal life.

Trevor

Becoming independent...

You have much to look forward to — moving away from home, meeting new colleagues and friends, and learning skills to form the basis of your career.

This transition can bring challenges. There's the wrench of leaving friends and family, and, for some at least, homesickness. For most though, these effects can be softened by becoming active in the new environment; keeping so busy that there's little time to dwell. But that comes with another challenge: to manage your time, so what has to be done does get done when it has to be done.

And there's the need to take responsibility for your decisions and actions without the immediate support that was available when at high school and home. That — taking responsibility and becoming independent — seems to me to be one of the most important changes between high school and university, and the one that most often causes problems. I hope it will not be an issue for you but will explain a little just in case.

These problems seem to be most common for young people who have had important decisions about what to do, how and when ('have you handed in that assignment yet...') made for them by well-intentioned parents, or by an over-supportive (usually expensive) school. Some of these schools seem to place more emphasis on the attainment of grades than on developing the skills of independent learning and in so doing place their students at a disadvantage

Many of those students are lost when they come to university and find that they alone must ensure that they learn and follow all rules and instructions, and fulfil the requirements of their courses. Some of them fail. I hope this will not happen to you but thought that I should draw your attention to this potential problem, and suggest a solution. It goes like this:

1. Accept that you (not your parents, even if they continue well-intentioned but counter-productive meddling) must accept responsibility, and act accordingly.

2. Get organised and develop systems. To do that it is necessary to check the relevant websites, attend the relevant introductory classes and develop a timetable listing what has to be done, how and when. And keeping a record of exactly what has to be done in each course, some of which have specific requirements about attendance and assessment — and making sure that follow those requirements.

3. Work out how to find and make effective use of course materials in the ways required for university-level courses. Forget relying on the spoon-feeding of school. Learn how best to use online and other resources, to complete tutorial presentations and other assessments in the form required, and to take advantage of other opportunities provided to learn these skills. The opportunities will be provided; it is up to you to take advantage of them.

I know that some of your colleagues will claim that these early classes are only 'introductory' (i.e. basic or 'easy') and that they can better use that time 'chilling' or socialising — or sleeping. Unfortunately, they will not know what they missed and what skills they failed to learn until it's too late, and they may fail.

Part of the reason for their failure is encapsulated in this quote from one of my textbooks on educational psychology: *The most important thing influencing learning is what the learner already knows.*

The reason that this is important is because it emphasises the importance of building the learning of a topic progressively from basic principles.

Those students who claim that sleeping, socialising, or 'chilling' should take preference over attending earlier classes usually do not realise what they miss: the principles on which the more practical applications will be built. Some of them wait until the more serious, detailed, 'practical' stuff comes along, and some base their final learning around past exam papers. Then, if the examiner deviates from the previous pattern of exam questions, these students bleat about how unfairly they have been treated.

At that time they usually do not realise that the real problems are yet to come — when they are in the workforce and faced with applications of the basic principles — those that they felt were too basic (or something like that) to bother with as students, and then found themselves unprepared.

If they had ensured that they knew the basic principles well, and based each step of their education on what they had already learned, they should have had the wherewithal to reason out exam questions that varied from previous patterns, and to solve work-related problems based on those principles.

That's the reason why we emphasise the importance of keeping on top of course material from the outset. It doesn't take a lot of time, especially in earlier year courses, but makes the learning process so much smoother, and usually more enjoyable. And the outcomes both in exams and work are better.

There's another, related point: some of your colleagues will claim that they do not need to attend the classes as they can get it all online. That's okay if it is online and they do use the online resources. Many don't — believe me.

And, as I'll explain later, those who attend a 'good' (and sadly they are not all 'good') class can learn much more than that they do online, especially if they write notes. The process of engaging with lecture material to convert the spoken word into written notes can establish at least the beginning of a structured memory, and make it easier to learn more thoroughly later.

In addition, an effective teacher conveys an attitude towards the material, and that is 'learned' at least to some extent by their students. A positive, engaging, inquiring, attitude, coupled with relevant examples and illustrations, can be picked up by students more or less unconsciously, resulting in greater interest and a more complete understanding. This also makes the task of learning the topic more appealing — and successful.

But, you may well say, I want to live my life and to enjoy my time at university. I would answer emphatically: you can do all that I have proposed and still have plenty of time for other pursuits. I am convinced that any student who can gain entry to a reputable university has the ability to develop and use the skills of independent learning, and to satisfy the requirements of their course, while still having time for sporting, social, cultural and other activities.

All that's needed is to develop a balance. My preferred way to do this is by being organised, creating a (realistic) timetable including everything: eating, sleeping, sport, socialising and 'chilling' as well as course requirements and other activities — and to sticking to it. I found it helpful to take one more step: keeping a record of the number of effective hours of course-related work each week. That provided a semi-objective measure of progress and had a positive effect on both conscience and motivation.

... Back to the beginning: the transition to university does involve many adjustments, many of which involve accepting personal responsibility but it is possible to make all those successfully and to have a brilliantly enjoyable, satisfying life at the same time.

I hope you can, and I will be cheering as I watch the transformation.

Trevor

Making the best use of time...

I suppose you are getting organised and working out how to balance your time between your studies and those other activities that look so appealing.

As I have watched successive generations of students, I have been impressed by how some achieve high grades while still enjoying the fruits of university life. Conversely, I have been concerned for others where the balance is tipped far in one direction (more fruits, lower grades) or other (high grades but few other fruits). I've concluded that some fairly simple things can help achieve a happiness-inducing balance between grades and fruits, and I thought I'd pass them on. Here goes:

Stay motivated, stay up-to-date. Motivation is an elusive quality, easily quenched but often hard to regain and retain. I've found it is much easier to stay motivated if it is possible to see where new material fits with that covered previously, and to progressively build up an overall understanding of the subject area.

It is easier then, to become interested, engaged, even intrigued, by the story as it unfolds, and that this generates the motivation to continue. I've also found that it is easier to stay up-to-date if well organised, working efficiently, staying fit and healthy. A few words about each point:

Be organised. Draw up a timetable with class times and other commitments, and set aside time for assignments and study, and for some balancing activities, especially exercise. Bear in mind that the study time is likely to be most effective when feeling fresh, and in a place without distractions.

Compile an assessment timetable, making sure you give enough lead time for each piece of assessment, especially those with similar end-dates. Then print the class and assessment timetables and put them in a prominent place, where they will act as a reminder, and remember to update them periodically to include any changes.

Having set out the timetable — *follow it.* Go to all classes unless experience shows that they are worthless and the material is available elsewhere — and then make sure that you use that material. Remember that if you attend the class, the material will pass through your brain at least once, and you'll find out what slant the lecturer puts on the material. That is critically important *because it is the lecturer who sets exams and is responsible for marking.* Another point — those who miss classes seem to find it easier to stay away because going back reminds them how much they have fallen behind.

Work as efficiently as you can. Ensure your working conditions are as good as possible and distractions minimal. Think about whether you work best in your room or a library, or some other quiet place. Try to avoid distractions from television and games etc., and from other people. Remember: *the more efficiently the work is done, the more time is available for other activities.*

Look after yourself. Put exercise, diet and sleep into the mix with study, sport and socialising. It is hard to maintain concentration and even good health if sitting down for long periods. Do regular exercise: sport, gym, swim.

Believe in yourself. Don't worry what others seem to be doing or to know. A lot of students seem to worry about this sort of thing, so I will deal with it in another letter.

If you need help, ask. If you've tried and failed to understand or to solve, ask the lecturer or one of your tutors. That's what they are there for.

In summary then, my best suggestions are to *go to classes, be organised, be efficient, be yourself.*

Trevor

Learning without even trying...

You've settled into your course, and are (I hope) learning a lot from your teachers. Probably, though, you are learning less than they hope they are teaching you. Conversely though you are also learning more than they think they are teaching you, and doing so without either you or your teacher being aware of it.

It is easy to overlook how much we learn just by observing, even unconsciously, how lecturers go about their craft. Their enthusiasm or lack of it, the clarity, focus and purpose they project, the examples and illustrations they use, all convey messages about their attitude to the topic.

That rubs off on us, the audience, and influences our own attitudes to the material, and potentially the whole subject.

My point is that we all learn a whole lot without even being aware of it, and often without trying. This type of learning is often referred to as 'implicit', to differentiate it from explicit learning: that which we are conscious of storing — or trying to store — in the memory. Implicit learning has a major influence on who we are and what we do, and on our attitudes to so many things. You may see the terms 'tacit' or 'unconscious' to refer to this type of learning, but don't feel confused; for our purposes they are the same.

You may ask: how does this apply to me and my studies? My answer is that it applies in many, many ways. I'll start with lectures, and in particular about whether going to lectures is a waste of time or not. Certainly they can be a bit of a waste of time if their only role is seen as transmitting information — as dictation lessons.

But, as I've mentioned previously, this need not be the case. An engaging, dynamic lecturer, for example, can generate a spirit of enquiry and a positive attitude to the material and of its relevance and application to the broader picture. That, to me, is at least as important as transmitting the 'facts' — and you — the students — may not even realise that it is happening.

Sadly, often from ignorance, this implicit learning is often overlooked by those who advocate replacing older teaching methods with technology.

Similar arguments apply to practical teaching situations. I will use an example from my field of veterinary anatomy. Traditionally, students of anatomy learned the relationships of structures to one another by dissecting them. But some have argued that these can be learned more efficiently from a computer image of someone else doing the dissection.

What these advocates overlook is that while dissecting, students learn much more than just where the bits are located, and much of what they learn they do unconsciously. For example, they develop skills in observing, in using instruments, and in handling tissues, as well as communicating and collaborating with colleagues dissecting that specimen, working together to achieve a specific outcome; all skills that they will need later as clinicians.

They also develop attitudes to working carefully and respectfully with body parts— attributes that are really important for those in medicine.

Similar issues apply to 'work experience' — spending time in a relevant workplace. Some students complain about this requirement, but do not realise is that this provides them with the opportunity to learn — often implicitly — how members of their future profession feel about and go about their business: how they interact with their clients and colleagues, confront and solve problems in the field, display appropriate (or less appropriate!) professional ethics, and generally comport themselves as professional people — in addition to the more technical aspects of the profession. So important!

While the curriculum may have (or may not have) included some formal instruction on these topics, I found that it was by seeing them in practice and observing the consequences of those actions that the important messages stayed in my mind.

You may hear your teachers say that this or that practical experience had to be discontinued either because it will be replaced by technology and/or was too expensive. The really sad thing when that happens is that students move to their later years not knowing (and their teachers not knowing) what skills their forerunners had learned implicitly; not knowing what could have been.

On another tack: some of your colleagues will complain about having to work to support themselves financially. Much of this work is in bars, restaurants, servos, call centres and the like, and these students learn — implicitly — how to deal effectively with the many potentially-stressful situations that arise while dealing with the public. For example, my field of expertise, veterinary science, involves working with people in what are often difficult situations, and employers have told me that when employing recent graduates, they prefer those who have had to work for money because they are likely to have learned valuable (implicit) skills and attitudes not taught in the curriculum.

As I've implied, many attitudes are learned, or at least modified, unconsciously by watching the behaviours of others (often those in a position of power and/or respect) and the consequences of those behaviours. This learning by observation is often so much more effective than words.

I remember well a situation where a group of student leaders exhorted a group of 'freshers' to, among other things, respect their colleagues, but then behaved in a disrespectful way. Not surprisingly, their actions were much more powerful than their words, and there was a danger that an atmosphere of disrespect would pervade the whole student population.

Each of us, whatever our level of seniority or status, influences others by what we do and how we do it, and how we say what we say (even if we say little), and will probably not realise the effect we are having. We can only hope that our behaviour influences them in a positive direction. Worth some serious thought, eh?

So, while we often learn less than we could (leading to the need to cram before exams), we also learn much more than we set out to learn. When interacting with others, when engaging in sports and other activities, we are absorbing cues and clues unconsciously. These interact with other stuff stored in the recesses of our memory and enable us to develop, or refine, the aptitudes we need to perform the various acts of mind and body that contribute to our ability to function as a person, whether as a student, a member of the workforce or of the general community.

You might now ask, *how does that apply to me, now?* My answer is that while it is important as a student to learn those things that are specified explicitly by your teachers, it is equally important to put yourself into situations where you can learn implicitly the relevant skills and desirable attitudes that will enable you to operate successfully in the workplace.

These learning situations may be in sporting, social, cultural, caring or other areas where those attributes are demonstrated and valued. In other words, it's not enough just to sit at the desk/computer and study, but equally important to get out and about, and learn how the world really works. But as with so many things in life, it is essential that these all be in balance with one another.

I hope you can achieve that balance and use both explicit and implicit learning to acquire the attitudes to become a well-rounded, highly respected potential member of your profession.

I'll do anything I can to help you work towards that objective.

PS After writing this letter I read the book 'Blink' by Malcolm Gladwell, the wise man who introduced *Tipping Point* into our language. He gives many examples of what he refers to as 'the power of thinking without thinking' and complements many of the points that I've raised here.

Trevor

Staying abreast...

I understand you're feeling a bit overwhelmed, so thought I'd offer a few suggestions. Firstly (and to repeat): be organised, use non-class time efficiently, and stay up-to-date. And:

1. *Divide the work into bites,* each of which can be managed in a single session. Most of us feel a bit overwhelmed when faced with a great mountain of work, especially if it seems difficult. It's easy to think that it is too hard and/or too much and that we don't have the energy or inclination to tackle it now. The work then piles up, and the situation exacerbates.

   It need not be that way. I've found that if I divide a large task into smaller chunks, and start by attacking what looks to be the easiest part, I can begin to make progress, and that provides motivation to complete that chunk. This gives a sense of achievement, which provides the impetus to keep going, attacking progressively-harder chunks until the whole task is finished. Whew!!

2. *Set specific objectives for each study session.* When I sit down at my desk I try to be clear what I hope to achieve in that session. It may be a part of a larger task or include several smaller tasks. I find that this approach keeps me focused, and leads to a sense of satisfaction as I cross that item off my list. Try it; it does help.

   I'm often reminded of how powerful a motivator success can be. I remember fearing some topics because I thought they were beyond me, but when I made an effort to master them, I found them interesting and engaging. It did take some effort initially, but that effort felt worthwhile when the meaning and relevance became clear.

3. *Master the basic principles.* Many topics are built from basic principles, which form the base of a hierarchy of subordinate principles and concepts. These concepts cannot be fully grasped without a clear understanding of the principles on which they are based.

13

Many less diligent students come to grief because they do not stay abreast of the material from the outset. They then try to cram or rely on past exam papers, without realising that they do not have the wherewithal to reason through the problems from basic principles. They may think they have an understanding, but do not realise that this is no more than a superficial understanding, and that is of very limited value for solving more complex problems in exams, and in the workplace.

4. *Keep a record of the amount of effective work done.* This can be a great motivator: looking back over what was achieved and then forward to help plan what needs to be done. This helped me a lot.

5. *Maintain a balanced life,* with plenty of exercise. I'm sure you've found that regularly doing exercise that you enjoy helps both motivation and efficiency. Some people stop exercising when they feel pressured, without realising that exercising may have enabled them to achieve more.

You'll probably notice that some of your colleagues do well academically, and are also active in other areas — sport, music, clubs and so on, and you might wonder how they manage it all. I bet you'd find that they organise their studies and other activities, and work efficiently — and that they follow most of the points that I've mentioned.

I hope that these points will help you to whittle away at that mountain of work that was worrying you so much, and that you enjoy the experience.

Trevor

Believing in yourself...

I was sorry to hear that you feel that you work harder but know less than many of your colleagues. Many of them probably feel the same way but are afraid to admit it. My best advice is to believe in yourself and not worry about what others seem to know.

One reason for this advice is that those who boast about what they (think they) know are often bluffing — bluffing themselves and trying to bluff others. Some think they know things, but are wrong. Some think they know but do not know what they don't know. Some come out of exams saying that it was easy when other students like you anguish over how hard they found it.

That troubled me too. Although it's aeons ago, I still remember coming out of an anatomy exam that I found hard, to be met by a friend who said *'wasn't that easy?'* I was deflated and worried. What did he know that I didn't? Then the results came out — and I realised that he'd found it easy because he didn't know what he didn't know — that the questions demanded more than he even knew existed. After that I paid little attention to what others were saying and kept my own counsel.

I must clarify one point though: there are some students who seem to know more and aren't bluffing. They are the ones who are smarter and do well despite doing, or seeming to do, less work. There aren't many of them.

Most students who achieve do work hard and effectively. Some, however, do much of their work away from prying eyes — in the library between formal classes, for example. Some go further and make themselves noticed when out and about socialising, but then hide away and study at other times when many of their colleagues are slacking. Their secret is managing their time well and working efficiently and effectively.

Another point: Early on, I learned to pay little attention to rumours that this or that will or will not be on the exam paper. Both when I was a student and later when lecturing, I'd hear these stories and sometimes the lecturer's name was invoked to give the story credibility. But often those stories were wrong, leading to grief among those who placed too much faith in them.

How could this come about? One possibility is that the lecturer may have, wittingly or unwittingly, given a clue but then forgotten about it when setting the paper.

This is one reason why as a lecturer I never gave exam tips: I was worried that I'd forget about the tip when I set the paper, which may be weeks later. It is also possible that, for reasons known only to them, the lecturer was devious, deliberately laying a false trail. And another is that the rumour was started by another student for a bit of mischief. It happens.

Since then, I've heard many stories spreading through groups of students, and found later that most were wrong. So I decided that the safest thing was to assume that all such rumours were wrong unless there was compelling evidence that they had substance.

Back to the main point: don't place too much faith in any unsubstantiated exam 'tips'. Of course learn that material well, but do not do so at the expense of a more complete coverage of the subject.

So my best advice is not to allow yourself to be influenced by what others say or seem to do about their study or exams, but do your best to manage your time well, and work efficiently.

Be yourself; have confidence in yourself. That approach does work; I can recommend it.

Trevor

Catching up...

I was sorry to hear that you are still a bit behind, and are still feeling unsure about how to get on top of those masses of material. I've tried to give some pointers in previous letters, but will use this one to add a few I have found useful, especially when faced with a mass of work that seems indigestible.

I've mentioned before that I find it helpful to break larger tasks into smaller bites that can each be handled within a single session. However, that alone may not be enough, especially if the overall task is especially challenging.

In that case, I look for parts that seem easier, especially if they involve the underlying principles, and start there. I've found that mastery of this 'easier' material can provide the confidence and motivation to move on to more taxing parts. But, whatever approach you use, make sure that you understand the basic concepts and principles, as mastery of these will be necessary for tackling more complex tasks that you encounter either during the course or later in the workforce.

Another point — some students become fixated on getting a particular grade or award and focus on that outcome. I've noticed that this can have really negative effects if the outcome is not achieved. I prefer the opposite approach: concentrating on the material for its own sake and trying to see where it fits into the larger picture, including the workplace. Focusing on the relevance, applicability and place of the material in the overall subject area makes it much more interesting and so easier to maintain motivation — and usually results in better grades.

I know that this is much easier to say than to do, but I have tried it both years ago as a student, and more recently when trying to force complex material into an unreceptive brain. I know too, from watching friends, how distressing it can be if the focus is on a particular grade (or award too) and that is not attained.

Think again about whether you are working in the best possible environment for effective studying. Ask: Is this the best location/room? Is the desk and chair at the best height for me; can I read the computer screen without straining my eyes; is the lighting satisfactory? And do I have easy access to all that I need, and can I find it when I need it?

Then: is this the best place to avoid distractions, either self-imposed — games, social media or loud music — or external distractions? If the answer to any of these is NO, make the necessary changes locally, or find another, better, place to work. This could be somewhere on campus: for example, a quiet corner in a library can be conducive to effective, uninterrupted study.

I know that these points seem obvious, but it is amazing how many people take their marginally satisfactory, environment for granted, and do not think about how it could be changed to help their learning.

And finally, check and recheck the official timetables and your timetables to ensure you have set aside enough time to cover all the course requirements and to prepare for the exams while continuing to live a balanced, low stress, enjoyable life. Achieving that balance is possible, believe me!!

If you think it is unnecessary to pay special attention to all these more-or-less mechanical details, then look further forward and see this as developing skills for the workforce. Most professional positions require competence in planning and meeting deadlines, and the transition to the workforce will be easier and more effective if these skills are well developed in advance.

I hope these extra points are of some help, and that you can enjoy mastering the material as you prepare for the exams — and for the workforce.

Trevor

Being assessed...

So it's assessment time again, with both progressive assessments (tute papers, mid-semester exams, assignments, prac write-ups etc.) and final exams on your agenda. What can I tell you that might be helpful?

Although it might seem fairly obvious, it is worth mentioning that assessment plays more than one role in education. The more obvious role — summative assessment — is to determine whether the objectives for the course have been met; whether the student has passed the course.

But at least as important is 'formative' — progressive — assessment, in which the student receives feedback to help them learn what is required. Although you probably had plenty of this at school, you may find that your university teachers vary a lot in the amount, timing and usefulness of feedback that they give on items of progressive assessment. That, as you may have found already, can be frustrating.

When working towards pieces of assessment, it is essential to plan ahead, if only to avoid stress. As I've suggested earlier, draw up a timetable that includes each piece of assessment, with some indication of the lead-time needed for each. This is especially important if several pieces are due at about the same time. Then it is important to pay attention to the relative importance of each piece, both in terms of what you can learn from it and the marks assigned to it.

If you have final exams, pay particular attention to planning your preparation, bearing in mind when each exam is scheduled, and following that plan (unless and until other factors dictate modifications to the plan). And think about where you can work best, preferably remote from friends, phones, computer games or other distractions, and in a place where the lighting, temperature and desk/chair combination give the best chance of working in the most effective and efficient way.

As I've mentioned in a previous letter, don't be spooked by a large mass of material, but divide it into chunks that can be managed in a single session, and start with the easiest. Then you can build up momentum to deal with the harder bits.

When thinking about the sequence in which you will attack the material, make sure that you master the basic principles before taking on material that is based on those principles. Otherwise, you may struggle, and not be able to work out why.

Also set (realistic) goals for each study session, and try to make sure that you achieve them before quitting. Also try to finish on a high note, when things are going well. That will make it easier to get started again after the break.

It is important also to stay fit and healthy: pay attention to diet, exercise and sleep (and noting the negative effects of some electronic devices on sleep). Some students let their fitness lapse and forget that they will probably work more efficiently and effectively if they make an effort to stay fit.

Now the task itself: the assignment, the exam. Most of my points are fairly self-evident, but you'd be surprised how many students need reminding. Here they are:

Check the instructions: make sure that you understand clearly what you are expected to do, both in terms of the instructions and the questions themselves. As part of this:

- *Check how much time is available;* check how many questions must be attempted and whether they are of equal value. Then calculate how much time should be spent on each, and be meticulous about staying within the time allocated.

  So often when marking, I've been saddened to find students spending too much time on earlier questions, leaving insufficient time for later questions, without realising that any extra marks accrued by going over time will almost certainly be lost if the final bell goes before they finish, especially if they leave out questions altogether.

- *Check what are you expected to do.* If you have to write your answer rather than answer multiple-choice or similar questions, pay special attention to the verb in the question: is it to describe, discuss, compare and contrast — or something else?

Then plan — in your mind if not on paper — what you intend to say and in what order to provide a clear, logical, complete and accurate answer. As you develop the answer itself, keep checking to make sure that you are (still) answering the question that was asked, and doing so as economically as possible.

And then develop your argument in a precise, concise form. Avoid unnecessary words, for they take time but yield no marks. Many students waste time by using unnecessary words (*i.e. 'at the current point of time'*, instead of *'now'*), or by including irrelevant material.

And remember to *attempt all questions*, even if you feel that you are bereft of clues about a question. Even a few words may earn those extra marks that you need.

Finally — and to repeat — check and check again to make sure that you do what is asked and within the designated time. For exams in particular, take steps to make sure that you:

- are at the right place at the right time, that you

- follow precisely the instructions on the paper, and that you

- provide a clear, logical and accurate answer to the questions asked (not the ones that you'd prefer to have been asked).

All this sounds blindingly obvious I know, but I stress the point because I've known too many students who have transgressed, and paid a high price. Please don't.

Trevor

Exams are over,
but what do you really know?...

Inoticed that your exam results are out, and was really pleased to see that you passed everything. But that prompted me to cogitate on what those results mean as a preparation for your future career.

That led me to think about what we know, where it may fit into the future workplace, and how we learn it. I thought it might be instructive to look at this under three headings:

- what we know and know we know;

- what we believe we know but don't really know, and

- what we know but don't know that we know.

What we know and know we know. That's the obvious one. The lecturer presents material, we learn it, regurgitate it in the exam, gain a pass, and are deemed to know enough to proceed to the degree and to use it in the work-place. But what if it is just a bare pass: 50%? Doesn't that mean that we don't know (or have not convinced the examiner that we know) up to one-half of the content, and what happens if later on we are called on to use that 50% in the workplace?

What we believe we know but don't really know is a logical extension of point 1. So often people believe that they know stuff, both in their formal courses and in life generally, but are fooling themselves.

Someone with but a superficial knowledge of a subject may think they have mastered it all but do not know what they do not know.

I mentioned in an earlier letter how I was taken aback by a colleague who believed that he had excelled in an exam that I found difficult, only to find that he gained much lower grade: he did not know what he did not know on the topics in the exam. I resolved then never to be concerned about comments about exams by other students.

This phenomenon — people believing they know more than they really know — is common, not only in university students but in the community generally. It has been shown to be behind major stuff-ups from plane crashes to major political disasters (including wars). It is called the Dunning-Kruger effect and is being studied by many psychologists; it would be worth following that up on the Internet.

What we know but don't know that we know. I mentioned this concept of implicit, (tacit or unconscious) learning in an earlier letter, but thought it worthwhile to draw your attention to its likely importance in navigating the changes that you'll encounter in your workplace(s).

This form of learning includes (but is certainly not restricted to) attitudes, skills in observation, creativity, perceptiveness, communication and other interpersonal skills.

Some of these can be learned from the teacher/lecturer. Even if they are not aware of doing so, these people convey an attitude to the material: if they sound bored, they will convey that attitude to their students: that the material is boring, even unimportant. Indeed, by paying attention to *how* they are saying *what* they are saying, their students can learn a lot more than just the content.

Specifically, we can learn how to communicate within that discipline, how the content can be applied in practical settings, the relative importance of different aspects, how to link various aspects in a creative way, how to implement a rigorous, analytical approach to questions and ethical issues.

I expect that you, like so many of your colleagues, will not attend lectures if they are likely to be a monotonous recitation of content, and will replace the lecturer with your computer screen. This is *so* sad, because attendance at classes, even dull ones, can at least give the feeling of some sort of communal learning experience, and also can encourage the taking of notes.

Even with a boring lecturer, taking notes by hand usually involves some intellectual engagement to produce an accurate summary, and this provides a skeletal framework for subsequent learning. By contrast, it has been shown that note-taking by keyboard is less effective as a basis for learning because most times this can be done with minimal cognitive engagement.

As I mentioned in an earlier letter, some implicit attributes are learned during practical classes, tutorials or during work experience. Unfortunately, many of these opportunities are being lost, some replaced by technology in the name of 'progress', and some discontinued because it is claimed, they cost too much. The really sad thing is that neither the perpetrators/administrators nor their students will ever know what learning opportunities the students have been deprived of; what could have been.

I often think about how much I learned during my work experience. Back then most veterinary students lived in the home of their 'supervisor' and spent most of the day (and often part of the night) in the car with them. Most of these practitioners were passionate about their role in and value to the community, and we absorbed a great deal of this positive attitude as well as attitudes to (and communicating with) clients, and the day-to-day operation of a practice/workplace.

We must have added to the (heavy) workload of our supervisors, but most undertook the task willingly, as they saw it as making a contribution to the future of their profession. They certainly did that, as we learned a great deal, much by implicit (i.e. unconscious) learning about how to behave, interact, and think as a professional person. And we absorbed (good or not-so-good) positions on moral/ethical aspects of professional work. It was by seeing these behaviours in practice and observing the consequences that we learned about them implicitly, and, I suspect, often uncritically.

I know I've laboured this point a bit, but it is very important. Many changes made to teaching/learning nowadays completely overlook the damage being made to the intuitive, more or less unconscious, learning of key attributes.

This is critically important because it is skills of this type that could enable you and your peers to adapt to changes in your workplace in future years. We all hear predictions about the number of professional jobs that will be replaced by technology. But there seems to be little doubt that those best able to adapt to such changes will be those with highly developed skills in rigorous original, critical, sceptical analytical thinking, insightful questioning, perceptive self-analysis, and the highest levels of ethics and integrity: many, many forms of higher-level (implicit) learning.

It is possible that artificial intelligence may help in learning some of these skills in future, but you and your peers will still need to rely on your own intelligence and critical thinking.

How you may ask, do I go about that? My best thought is to pay attention to what you can learn in any situation, then practising those skills, preferably with constructive feedback. This will involve having an expert, perceptive and willing 'coach' who may be a teacher, a boss, a colleague.

I hope these thoughts will help you be conscious of new learning opportunities and that you enjoy the experience.

Trevor

About Heads

Looking after *your* head

I've been getting a bit worried about you. I've tried to contact you several times recently but with no response. Then one of your friends mentioned that you had become a bit of a recluse, staying in your room in the dark, not going to classes and missing meals.

That made me anxious because a number of times over the years I've found that a friend showing that sort of behaviour is feeling especially low, fighting gremlins in his head but not knowing what to do. One of those friends had recently moved into a flat but was not answering his phone or responding to messages for several weeks. When I did eventually make contact, it was clear that his head was really misbehaving, and this was affecting his ability to study or to face the world.

When he first admitted that something was amiss, he found it impossible to say what was happening. After a while though, he was able to write about how it was affecting him and to accept help. He then received treatment for clinical depression from a psychiatrist and from a psychologist for social anxiety and is recovering.

This episode was troubling, especially when it emerged that he had been hurting for several years of our friendship and I had not noticed. I should have noticed because I have been fighting the gremlins of depression myself for many moons, and try hard to identify and help those similarly afflicted.

Those of us who are keen to help young people — and especially young males — realise that most are reluctant to talk about issues of greatest importance to them, whether these are family traumas, difficulties in relationships, sexual orientation — or mental health and ill-health.

Some do not seek help because they are unsure about what is happening or do not know where to seek help. Some are embarrassed to seek help because they are concerned about what other people — even family and close friends — will think. Nowadays, the stigmas around most of these issues are receding, but it is understandable that so many arent' keen to take the risk.

I've found that some young people are worried but are not sure whether the problem is real, or if they are imagining it. There are websites that will help by giving answers to questions about misbehaving heads, and even provide a self-test as a guide to whether to seek professional help. One reputable site is from the Black Dog Institute (www.blackdoginstitute.org.au), associated with the University of New South Wales in Sydney.

Another credible and informative site that you might find helpful is Beyond Blue (www.beyondblue-men.or.au) and, on the world stage, the World Federation for Mental Health (http://wfmh.com).

The Black Dog Institute website has, among other useful things, a description of Mindfulness, an approach involving meditation and self-awareness apparently derived from Buddhist practices.

If you have been feeling low for a couple of weeks or more, have lowered self-esteem, or low motivation or an inability to enjoy life, check these websites, especially the Black Dog one. If this convinces you that the gremlins have moved in, make an appointment with your University Health Service or family doctor, and they should help you find appropriate treatment.

They will also be concerned about your general health, and how well you are looking after yourself: diet, sleeping, stressors, and exercise, and may be able to give some help in these areas too.

Though a bit too lazy to be naturally attracted to exercise routines, I can attest to the value of exercise in promoting a feeling of wellbeing even when feeling depressed. But that is but a supplement to the ministrations of my psychiatrist.

I saw a very pertinent statement on the website of the World Federation for Mental Health, and thought it worth quoting:

> Treatment of depression is much more successful when the condition is diagnosed and treated early... Adequate treatment is a critical factor in reducing symptoms... half of those with depression do not get access to treatment either because they are not aware of the symptoms or because they are afraid to seek help due to stigma....

I understand this well because of my own long experience with depression. As I think back, I realise that for years I ignored the symptoms and would not admit even to myself that treatment was needed. But then circumstances forced me to accept help, and since then have been able to keep those pesky gremlins (of depression) at least partially under control.

Four things that have helped greatly are:

- **Regular exercise:** although I don't have much aptitude for sports, I gained a lot from playing squash regularly. This provided both regular exercise and social contact, as we'd sit and chat for a while after each game. For me organising to exercise with someone else provided the impetus to move.

- **Contact with nature:** since the ageing body told me to give up squash, I've taken to the bush several times a week, with long lens camera in hand.

- **Having a project:** setting an objective and then achieving it can provide a real boost. I do that mainly by trying to get the best possible photos of birds while exercising in the bush. That means that expeditions into the bush help in all three ways: exercise, contact with nature and working towards an objective, and can also lead to a sense of achievement if I achieve the objective — some decent photos.

- **Having a 'therapy' pet.** We've found that 'retired' greyhounds fill that role magnificently: in a quiet yet loyal way they can provide amazing support to a depressed person.

If you are unfortunate to be afflicted by depression, it is some consolation to know that you are in the company of some of the most eminent and creative people in history.

Don't you believe me? Well, just type in 'famous depressives' or something similar into your search engine, and you'll be surprised at the list. Some include moon-walking astronaut Buzz Aldrin, Harry Potter author JK Rowling, musicians Sting, Billy Joel and Elton John, and composers Beethoven and Tchaikovsky, and Princess Diana.

I know that it can be hard to admit to oneself that things are not right in the head. But it is easier to accept if that step is seen as one along a path of effective treatment, and that this will lead to removal of at least some (and I hope all) those troubling symptoms.

So I urge you to seek help if you feel that there's any chance that the gremlins of depression have invaded that magnificent head of yours.

Trevor ✑

So your friend has problems in his head...

I didn't expect to hear so soon that you have a friend who needs help and I was saddened by that news. I'm writing now to pass on a few more tips — tips that I've learned from almost a lifetime dealing with my own depression, and trying to help others similarly afflicted.

The most difficult part of helping someone can be for them to admit there's a problem. I remember a friend who seemed troubled, but it took three years of subtle trying (and at least one suicide attempt) before he agreed to seek help. By then, it was a bit late, and he's been unable to work for a couple of years — tragic.

That time I was not very successful in overcoming reluctance to seek assistance but have had more success with other friends. Things that have helped include:

- Working with them to get competent, congenial, professional help preferably involving an experienced, thoughtful, concerned, and wise psychiatrist and/or registered clinical psychologist, although a general practitioner with special aptitude and interest can also be of immense value. But note that not all GPs fall into that category.

It is essential that your friend feels comfortable with the practitioner. Unfortunately, not all mental health practitioners are equally competent, and not all are genuinely interested in mental health. Recently I heard from a good friend who was in two hospitals after a suicide attempt, and he felt that none of the four hospital psychiatrists who were assigned to him really seemed to care about him as a person. It was not until he consulted a fifth, outside the hospital environment, that he found someone with empathy and concern — and competence — who really seemed to want to help him.

- Supporting/encouraging them to do what the doctor tells them to do.

  Helping them identify any stressors to which they may be especially susceptible, so they can try to work around them, or avoid them altogether. We vary a lot in our susceptibilities; some people are especially sensitive to:

  - high risk situations;

  - confrontation or criticism;

  - a need to focus on details;

  - having to work towards tight deadlines;

  - assessments of any sort;

  - high or complex workloads...whereas others are immune to or even thrive under these conditions.

  Unfortunately, many of us do not pay enough attention to potential stressors, and, especially if genes add susceptibility, succumb. It is worth suggesting that your friend makes a real effort to identify things that cause them stress, and makes a conscious effort to try to avoid them. In the same vein, a list of things that have the opposite — positive — effect may help counter the effects of stressors.

- Try to find out about their involvement with drugs. The environments of many young people are awash with marijuana, and some 'friends' entice their colleagues to participate, claiming that it is harmless. Not so: the effects may be subtle, leading to reduced motivation (and exam grades), and it can lead to long-term effects, including schizophrenia.

  Not long ago I was asked to help a young person who had been using marihuana with his friends, and they all added a small amount of LSD. His 'friends' were not seriously affected, but he descended into a deep hole. He remained in his room, almost unable to function, for weeks. His 'friends' were reluctant to seek help because they feared the consequences that would follow the revelation of their own drug-taking. Eventually, it was possible to arrange for him to obtain treatment, but this involved several weeks in a psychiatric hospital. This made me even more alert to the need to consider drugs when confronted by a person showing problems in their head, but at least as important, to the possibility that this information may be withheld.

- Encouraging them to exercise regularly. Although people who are depressed may not feel motivated to exercise initially, they usually feel significant benefit if they can get started with and continue a routine that appeals to them.

- Encouraging them to take up a hobby or other activity that is within their competence and interest. If they can complete at least some part of this, it can give a sense of achievement, and that can motivate them to make it part of their regular routine.

- Point them to reputable websites such as:

  - www.beyondblue.org.au/resources

  - www.blackdoginstitute.org.au

- Being a supportive, non-judgmental, respectful, and confidential, 'friend'.

- Not becoming so personally involved as to compromise the ability to provide objective, constructively-helpful advice and support.

I'm really glad that you are planning to help your friend; I bet you'll be pleased you did. But if things do not work out, try not to feel guilty, but be content that you did your best for them. Do let me know if there's anything I can do to help.

Trevor

Can you blame your brain?

A few days ago your mother mentioned that she is worried that you've been taking more risks than she's comfortable with, and getting into some bother.

When she asked me what she should do about it, I suggested she wait a while and place faith in the values you'd learned during your early life, and wait for this phase to pass.

We all go through phases in our attitudes and behaviours throughout our lives, but there's no doubt that the exploratory phase of young adulthood — the one that you are in now — is one that gives many parents plenty to worry about. However, I felt that I owed it to her, and to you, to use my background in physiology and anatomy to try to come up with a more credible and convincing answer.

The answer is interesting and illustrates the value of modern technologies — in overturning old beliefs and providing some understanding of how young people's brains change, and so change their behaviour.

This is interesting to me because, like all life science students for generations, we were expected to tell examiners that no new cells are produced in the brain after birth. Now it is known that this is nonsense; our brains continue to produce new cells, especially early in life.

The problem is that different parts of the brain develop at different rates, and as a result, a mismatch occurs between the activities in different parts that interact with one another. Two of these parts are the limbic system, deep within the brain, and the prefrontal cortex, near the front.

What does each part do? The limbic system is the source of spontaneous, impulsive, emotion-driven behaviours, whereas the prefrontal cortex has a much more regulating, reasoning, logic-based role. To a large extent it is responsible for determining how the output of the limbic system is translated into action — into actual behaviour.

However, the limbic system develops first, stimulated at least in part by the hormones of puberty, whereas the prefrontal cortex develops more gradually, not reaching full regulatory activity until mid-twenties or later.

The end-result of the mismatch is that control over the impulsive activities initiated in the limbic system develops gradually, and will not reach full development for a few years, although the exact times do vary.

It would be tempting to blame bad behaviour by young people on this mismatch in the development of their brains, but this would be far too simplistic and does not absolve young people from responsibility for their actions. Furthermore, the control that does exist can be suppressed, often by alcohol or other drugs, allowing free reign to impulses generated by the limbic system. This can cause real problems with behaviour.

Don't be too despondent though, as the mismatch has positive aspects. These include the (apparently) spontaneous and impulsive behaviours that make many young people such bright and appealing personalities, prepared to 'have a go' with less regard to what 'people will think'.

But their developing prefrontal cortex will, over time help modulate risk-taking behaviours and give increasing ability to make 'mature' judgments.

However, it does take effort to keep those part of the brain in socially-acceptable balance. I hope that you will be able to exert that effort, and enable all those changes in your head to fit you for a rewarding and successful life.

But back to the original question: can you blame your brain? It would be easy to answer yes: that the mismatch in development is responsible for the behaviours that some adults find distasteful.

I prefer the opposite view: that the mismatch is responsible for much of the spontaneity and openness that makes people of your age and stage so interesting and appealing. I often feel a bit sad when I see that qualities become suppressed over time as a veneer of conformity reflects the increasing prefrontal control of advancing adulthood.

I hope that you are able to retain those good qualities as you move forward in your life and career. Like so many things in life, it's a matter of balance.

Trevor

On Interacting With Others

How well are you communicating...?

In an earlier letter, I mentioned that we learn unconsciously a lot of the skills that we use in communicating with other people. One obvious example of this is when little people learn to talk, but there are many others.

We are sending messages most of the time, even when we are not aware of it. Most messages that we send consciously are as words, but we also send messages by the words we select and how we package and send them, as well as how we dress, move and speak, and by our gestures, eye movements, facial expressions and more. Even though we may not be aware of it, all these convey information about what's going on in our heads.All of that is extremely important, not only in life generally but in professional work. As a student you will have learned many relevant skills by observing and thinking often unconsciously, but may not have become aware of the principles underlying these skills, or how they may be made more or less effective in different situations.

For aeons, it has seemed to me, that given the importance of communication in all professions, there would be great merit in providing students with some cognitive structures by which they could enhance the skills that they had acquired already. We all had that experience early in life when we were taught the structure of our language — spelling, grammar and so on — to enhance the speaking skills that we had learned implicitly.

But until fairly recently university courses in my profession and in most others did not provide any such instruction. Arguments for their introduction were met with derisive comments such as: 'that stuff is not suitable for a university course' or 'we all know those things already' (even though objective observation would reveal otherwise). But the real reason apart from educational apathy was often that the opponents feared that introduction of new material might be at the expense of time allocated to their topics. Where teaching time equated to academic power, this argument was difficult to counter, at least with logic.

Eventually logic and common sense won, and we were able to provide our students with some structure upon which to refine their skills in communicating with clients, colleagues and the community. And I'm pleased to report (but not to claim credit) such courses are now commonplace.

Here I'll try to convince you of the value of some formal learning to enhance what we learn intrinsically and so enable us to communicate more effectively.

I know I'm entering dangerous territory because those who comment on communication make themselves vulnerable to criticism about their own messages. So I'll make it clear that I have no pretentions about my skills in this (or any other) area, and welcome criticism when I transgress.

Although we may not think about it consciously, our objective in sending messages is presumably to convert our thoughts into a form that enables them to be received clearly, completely and precisely. That's a big order. It implies that we know exactly what message we want to send and can convert those thoughts into clear, unambiguous communication. Sounds obvious I know. But I often find that I only truly understand what I am thinking after I try to put this into words. Think: has that happened to you?

There's another key point here: having put the thoughts into words it is worth asking: should I send this message, or a different message or no message. This is relevant in the current climate where messages can be created and sent in such a spontaneous, instantaneous way, and once sent, cannot be retracted. What I try to do when tempted to fire emotion-laden verbal bullets, has been to neutralise the emotions by writing a draft, then letting a day or two pass before deciding whether and what to send.

It is also worth thinking carefully about the likely impression that the message will create in the receiver, and how this may be affected by (a) the words that are used and (b) the way the words are arranged and presented.

As part of this process, I ask myself whether the intended meaning could be conveyed more clearly. Then: is it clear and precise, would it be easier to understand if more succinct, does it convey the right emotional flavour, does it adhere to the principles of English grammar wherever possible; is it direct, in the active voice as in: 'we won tennis rather than tennis was won by us.'?

Then I'd seek and destroy unnecessary words (such as in 'at the current point in time' instead of 'now') and imprecise, meaningless terms such as several, many, various, or jargon, acronyms, clichés and other trendy terms that may cause confusion or frustration.

On that line, I've just read a piece by linguist Roly Sussex called 'Going forward, just sunset the business lingo' bemoaning the overuse and misuse of ordinary words like 'conversation' 'journey' and 'reaching out' to the extent that they become clichés and cease to have a clear meaning.

Next step: how to send it? That depends on the purpose of the message. For example, if you hope to convince the recipient that they are dealing with a credible, professional source, pay special attention to the font and formatting, to the letterhead and to the quality of the paper if it is to be printed. Or if you hope to convince somebody of your enduring love and affection, you are likely to have more success if the visual impression of the letter — or whatever form of transmission you use — matches the words.

I find that the best way to write something that conveys my meaning clearly (or as clearly as I can manage) is to make a draft that conveys the ideas and then refine it in a series of revisions. Each time I go through the text I ask myself: does this word or sentence convey my meaning exactly or can I do better; can it be expressed more clearly or concisely; is it in the best place?

And then, when it all appears okay, I check it rigorously. For each word, phrase, sentence and paragraph I ask: is it necessary (and if in doubt cut it out), is it accurate, is it clear? And then check it again, searching specifically for errors. This might sound obsessive, but I find that even after all this checking, I usually find an error or something I'd like to change after it is too late to make a change. So I've learned to check one more time.

I should mention here the spell-checkers and predictive programs that try to second-guess our meaning. As I'm sure you have found, they can get it badly wrong, creating nonsense or worse. To my later annoyance, I find that I can overlook those errors if reading with a view to what I expect to find rather than specifically looking for errors (and there is a difference). Sometimes it is worth getting another set of eyes to double-check.

I hope I have conveyed my thoughts clearly, and that they will be useful as you strive to convey your thoughts so that they are received clearly and without difficulty or distortion.

Trevor

Communication involves much more than just words...

I'd like to expand a bit on some points I mentioned in the last letter, and ask: what really happens when we speak to another person?

The words themselves are certainly important, but we convey additional meaning by the way we say them, by the speed, pitch and loudness and also by the emphasis we put on individual words.

But we do even more than that: we also send part of the message in non-verbal ways, and this often happens without us realising what we are doing. These nonverbal cues include our eye movements, facial expressions, gestures, by whether we adopt a confronting or more relaxed posture, and by what we wear and how we wear it.

The way we dress conveys strong messages: uniforms imply authority, white coats imply professional expertise, and so on. I have clear memories from an earlier incarnation of a secretary who occasionally gave me a dressing down about something I'd done or not done. And every time she did that she arrived wearing the same cream pantsuit. So if she came in that outfit I knew to take cover!!

Taken together these nonverbal parts of the message can modify, or even negate, the apparent meaning of the words themselves. So it is important to pay close attention to the nonverbal as well as the verbal components of the message if we are to understand clearly the message that was in the mind of the other person.

Another point: some people keep the most important parts until late in a message, so it is important to hear — not just listen casually to — the whole of the message and not to jump to conclusions before the end. I well remember a senior colleague who would phone and initially engage in casual conversation of varying length, and I had learned to be patient for the bombshell that he was about to drop because the size of the potential bombshell was directly proportional to the length of the (usually irrelevant) preamble.

I know that this all sounds a bit complex, especially for casual chitchat. But there will be times when the message is so important that it is worth listening actively to the words and how they are said, observing carefully for nonverbal cues and then thinking consciously and critically to integrate the material from these various sources. This should give you the best chance that the message that you receive will be the same as the one that was in the mind of the sender.

I've found that this is all most likely to happen if I pay overt attention to psychological comfort. If it is likely that the issue will be sensitive or potentially embarrassing, I try to find somewhere where we will not be distracted, where both of us are likely to feel at ease (such as sitting at a slight angle to one another but not in their personal space, and without any barriers such as a desk), by sitting in a relaxed position (and not having arms crossed), and looking at the other person's face and eyes, not staring, and not glancing around the room in a distracting way.

You might think this is a bit contrived, but if you think about those people you are most comfortable having a personal chat with, you will probably realise that they do these things more or less automatically. You probably do too, but you might give a little more thought to ensure that they become part of your persona. That should help a lot to ensure that you send and receive your messages accurately.

I know I'm far from perfect in this (as in everything), but am still trying…

Trevor ⬤⟜

Conveying meaning in writing...

The idea of writing about letter writing came to me when I was listening to the radio, and they played a piece with the intriguing title of *The lost art of letter writing*, by local composer Brett Dean. He apparently wrote it because of a concern about (as he wrote): 'the heavy reliance on electronic stimuli in his daughter's education, and that we are losing touch with the tactile element of written communication.'

That prompted me to think about my experience with letters. For most of my life they have been the main way to send written messages, and have worked hard to try to convey the precise message that I intended.

Nowadays most people get little practice, and virtually no instruction, in the craft of writing messages that convey both a precise literal meaning and something of the attitude of the writer to the topic and the recipient. I'm reminded of this often when I read communications on my screen or on paper.

I don't mean to be critical about your emails, texts or Facebook Messages, but will offer a few clues in the hope that they will be helpful in the future. One thing that I do urge you to do is to try to see the message from the point of view of the person reading it, and to ask yourself: what can I do to make sure that the reader will receive the precise message that I am trying to convey? Here are a few ways that I've found to help bring that about.

Consider the emotional tone that you hope to transmit — stern, neutral, persuasive, friendly, loving — and make sure that the words are consistent with this tone. Many writers of official letters fail on this count. For example, I receive some letters that start with an attempt at friendliness — Dear Trevor — but continue with some unpalatable, and often obtuse, officialese that creates an impression that is far from friendly. The overall impression is one of insincerity or worse. They go straight to the bin.

Address it to a real person, not some nameless 'Sir/Madam' or 'To Whom it may Concern'. This can imply that their name is not important; usually a big mistake. An effort made to find out the real name of the person holding an official position will generally be repaid by the greater attention that your message will receive.

Pay particular attention to wording, grammar, setting out and visual impression generally. This is important to convey the impression — I hope correctly — of a credible professional source. If it does not do this, there is the risk that it, together with any attachments such as a job application, may be consigned to the bin.

Start the message with a clear, concise and precise statement of the reason for writing. For example, if applying for a job, say so. Don't use indirect expressions like 'I am interested in applying for a job', for this begs the question: if interested in applying, why not apply? Say what you mean, unambiguously.

Then convey the message in direct and clear, but courteous and respectful, language. If pasting in material from other sources, ensure that it is consistent with the meaning and tone of the rest, and makes sense.

In the final para summarise the points that you want the reader to concentrate on, mention any attachments such as a resume, and any further actions that may be needed — such as availability for an interview.

If you need to sign it, do so legibly. Illegible, bank-type signatures may be OK for the most formal of letters, but I believe that a legible signature — one that indicates some respect for the recipient, can increase the chance of a positive response.

You might think that these points belong to an earlier time and no longer apply. My point is that they are still worthwhile if they help to convey both the literal and emotional meaning clearly and accurately from your mind to that of the reader. I hope you will feel able to implement them, and find them helpful.

Trevor

Writing for publication: The principles...

I was pleased to hear that you have been asked to prepare a manuscript in the hope of having it published. I'd like to pass on a few things I've learned during decades of writing for the scientific and educational literature, and hope they help.

The objective in any such writing should be to convey your message to the mind of the reader in a clear, unambiguous and engaging way. Sound pretty straightforward, but there are many facets to consider.

Firstly, know exactly what you want to say. Ensure that your information, whether from other people's papers or from your own work, is accurate and that you know precisely the meaning and the interpretation that you want to convey. You may find that you will modify some of your views as you struggle to understand and interpret different points, and to put them into words. But before you have finished, you should know clearly what you are trying to say; if you are not, your readers will be even less clear.

Secondly, be precise. Strive to convey your meaning accurately with the smallest number of precise yet simple words.

Keep sentences short. It is easy for a reader to be confused by a long sentence, especially if it is not well constructed.

Use simple language. Long and complex words do not imply greater wisdom than simple words with the same meaning. But they are more confusing, especially to readers who are not expert in that subject. Thus most people would find it easier to understand 'ear, nose and throat specialist' than 'otorhinolaryngologist'; 'place in alphabetical order' than 'alphabetise', and so on.

Resist the temptation to use jargon or complex technical terms when simple words will do. Say 'cause of an eye disease' rather than 'aetiology of an ophthalmological disorder'; 'the bull was killed' rather than 'the male bovine was euthanased or sacrificed, or horror of horrors, euthanatised)' and so on.

I suggest that when you have written a draft, then check each long, complex, excessively technical and/or pompous-sounding word and ask yourself: can I say this more simply? For example, can I use 'horse' for 'equine', 'see' for 'visualise', 'use' for 'utilise', 'high' for 'elevated', or 'about' for 'approximately'? As a final check, ask: would it be understood by someone for whom English is a second language?

Use words in their exact meaning. If in doubt about the meaning of a word, look it up. If still in doubt, try another word; check a thesaurus for a word that does convey your meaning accurately.

Avoid imprecise words. For example, quantitative words such as considerable, considerably, substantial, substantially, appreciable, appreciably, very, much and more, often do not convey a clear meaning and should be avoided where possible.

Avoid complex adjectival groups. Some writers, in an effort to be concise, string together a group of words before a noun, as in 'abnormal serum enzyme liver function test'. This can be confusing, and it is worth adding a few more words to make the meaning clear: 'abnormal level of serum enzymes used in liver function testing.'

Avoid pompous and long-winded expressions such as 'at the current point of time' for 'now'; 'of profound theoretical and practical importance' for 'important'; 'in a considerable number of instances' for 'often' ... and so on.

At an early stage, find and follow the style and Instructions to Authors of the target journal. As you will have seen, papers in most journals are organised so that the reader is presented with, in order:

1. *The title,* which is the first thing that is read, and plays a key part in determining whether the reader will read on. It is also the basis for indexing and information retrieval, so the words should be chosen with great care, and arranged so to give a clear, comprehensive yet concise and engaging picture of what the paper is about.

2. *A list of authors* and their affiliations;

3. *An abstract*, which is a summary of the key points that will appear in the paper;

4. *An introduction* to the topic and its significance and how it is to be discussed;

5. *A description of the methods* or procedures used;

6. *The results* of the study in a logical, well-argued sequence. Results and discussion are usually separate in original scientific papers but may be combined in other publications. Thus in a review of literature, it is common for the results obtained by other workers to be discussed when they are first presented to the reader.

7. *A summary* of the key points and conclusions. If the paper is short and deals with one main theme, a single concluding statement may suffice. But for longer and more complex pieces of writing it is usually helpful to the reader if the argument is drawn together at the end of each theme, with a final summing-up at the end.

8. *A list of references* to papers cited in the text (and no others). When reference is made to the work of others, this should be acknowledged in the text at the appropriate place, and full bibliographic details given, usually at the end of the paper, in the style specified. In the social sciences, it is common to list references in footnotes, but footnotes are not commonly used in scientific publications. Programs such as Endnote make citing and listing references pretty straightforward.

9. If the paper includes *Tables and/or Figures*, they should:

   • be clear and as simple as possible, containing only essential information, and be self-explanatory without reference to the text;

   • have a clear and concise headings/captions that are restricted to information that is necessary to understand the figure or table;

   • each is mentioned in the text, with an outline of what they represent, and what conclusions can be drawn from them.

10. *Units.* Most journals require that the International System of Units (SI) be used and that those units be represented by standard symbols.

11. *Abbreviations.* These should only be used where necessary such as for SI and related units and for long technical terms especially if they are repeated many times. Abbreviations for technical terms other than

those covered by SI symbols and any specified by the journal should be spelt out when they first appear, with the abbreviation in parentheses; for example, Grade Point Average (GPA). Whatever abbreviations are used should be consistent throughout the paper.

12. *Numbers.* In general, numerals are used when followed by a standard unit of measurement (such as 8 km, 29 g) and for times (1.00 pm), dates (4 Jan. 1937), percentages (8%), decimal numbers (0.121) and page numbers (p 5). Numbers one to nine should be spelt out, but numerals used for higher numbers. An exception: a number starting a sentence should be spelt out.

13. *Tenses.* These cause many headaches for authors. I have found it best to use past tense for experimental methods and observations (e.g. Joe Blow (1974) observed that ...), and present tense for established knowledge (e.g. 'man has a brain'). And to be consistent.

14. *Exclusive publication*: a paper can only be published once. Journals require that papers submitted to them not be published, or under consideration, by another journal.

15. *Plagiarism and the infringement of copyright.* In general reference to the work of others is considered legal and ethical if (a) it does not consist of a direct reproduction of, say, a figure or table, or the direct quotation of more than a few lines unless specific written permission has been obtained from the holder of the copyright (usually the publisher or the author), and (b) the source is acknowledged. This is usually done by inclusion in the reference list, but if specific permission has been obtained from the copyright holder, this should be acknowledged.

Trevor ●◆

Writing for publication: The process...

I hope the last letter gave you some useful background; now for the writing itself. There are many differences in writing behaviour, but this is how I've gone about it.

Organise the material

- Start with that which is most easily organised; for an original scientific paper this is likely to be the Materials and Methods and the Results.

- Develop a series of headings for the various sections of the work. These headings may be discarded as the writing progresses, but they do help organise the material into a logical sequence. Under each heading, fill in the information in rough form. This will help you to decide whether you do have enough to develop and support your arguments, and which, if any, should be presented in figures or tables.

- Draft out the figures and tables, trying alternative forms until you are satisfied that they are clear, complete and easy to understand. When this is done you will be in a better position to compile the text.

Decide on the precise form of the paper

- If writing for publication, decide which journal you will submit to, then consult both the Instructions to Authors and recent issues of the journal, then follow these precisely.

- If writing an essay or report and no specific instructions have been given, you should decide how the paper will be divided under headings and subheadings, and follow a consistent pattern. For references, tables, figures abbreviations and so on — select a prestigious journal in that field and follow their conventions.

Write a complete rough draft

- Concentrate on developing a coherent, logical story; the details of style and form can be taken care of in later drafts. I suggest adhering to the formal requirements of the journal and keeping a record of references from the start; you are then less likely to have errors in the final copy.

Let the ideas incubate for a while

- Put the draft away for a few days so that your subconscious mental processes can work on it at leisure. When you come back to it you will probably bring fresh insights and a more critical and constructive approach; the task will be easier and the product better than if you had worked on it without a break.

Rewrite, concentrating on structure, then on style

- Pay particular attention first to the overall structure of the story you are telling, and to the logical presentation of its parts.

- Then, in relation to each part — sentence, paragraph, section, heading, figure, table — ask yourself: is this:

  - necessary; does it contribute to the story, or should it be deleted?

  - correct and accurate; have I checked the original source?

  - in the best place; would re-ordering make the story clearer and more logical?

  - presented in the best way: or could the point be made more clearly and precisely?

Seek feedback from both experts (supervisor and/or colleagues) and non-experts. Then consider their comments, incorporate those that make sense, then check, and check again that the manuscript is in the form required, then send it off.

If sent to a reputable journal, it will be sent to expert referees, who will report to the editor who will respond by (a) accepting it, possibly with minor changes or (b) require major changes based on the referees' reports, or (c) not accept it but will consider a revised version, or (d) reject it.

I hope yours will be accepted, and you will soon see your work in print.

PS: I found this book to be authoritative, clear and very helpful: Seely, John Oxford *Guide to Effective Writing and Speaking*. Oxford University Press, Oxford, 2013.

Trevor

Making and interpreting decisions: traps for the unwary...

Making and responding to decisions is central to all our lives, both personally and in professional work. And from time to time, we are faced with decisions that seem bereft of logic, sense or common sense.

That is a real concern, especially nowadays when, to an increasing extent, 'evidence' is being extracted from huge data sets, and used for decisions of great import. But although these decision-makers may justify their decision by pointing to the depth and breadth of the data used, this does not mean that the decisions are well based and flow logically from that set of data.

A similar concern is generated by claims that students do not now need to learn as much as they did in earlier times because they can just look it all up on the Internet. While they may be able to gain access to the 'facts', they may lack the wherewithal to make sound decisions based on those facts.

This is a topic I've mulled over much and realised that it has so many facets that I'll need to make this letter longer than usual if I'm to have any chance of being understood. Sorry about that.

A disclaimer: The topic is broad and my grasp of it limited. What I will try to do is to point to some issues that can derail decision-making wherever it happens.

Limiting the question: I'll start by asking three questions:

1. who is making the decision, and are they working alone or in concert?

2. who is affected: only the decision-maker, or others?

3. what is the basis of the decision: for example, is a decision to work with another party based (mainly) on:

   • emotion (I hate Mr A , so will not do business with him)

   • opinion (B is not a worthy person, so I will not....)

- personal preference (C is a friend of mine so I will …)

- perceptions of integrity (D has told lies in the past, so I will not…)

- evidence (E has offered convincing evidence, so I'm confident to…)

Given that the first four of these are subjective — not amenable to objective analysis — I will consider only those decisions based on objective evidence. But we should remember that decision-makers may be influenced by subjective factors even though their decision is presented as based on objective evidence. And that one of the most common subjective factors is self-interest. As has been said by many people: *if self-interest is in the race, back it every time.*

So what is evidence? Initially, we may ask: what do I already know, or can find out, about the topic? But that question is not clear-cut, because the verb 'to know' can be viewed in different ways. As discussed in a previous letter, 'knowing' can come in various forms. Thus we may:

1. know and know that we know;

2. think we know but don't really know;

3. know but don't know that we know;

4. don't know and know that we don't know, and

5. don't know and don't know that we don't know.

I'll try not to repeat too much from that earlier letter, but discuss each version of the verb 'to know' as it applies to decision-making.

1. What we know and know that we know
This seems pretty straightforward but, as set out below, we need to remember that our memory of what we 'know' can be faulty.

We must for example be sceptical about those things that we 'know' because we have learned them from other people. Ideally, this 'knowledge' would be relevant and accurate and derived from a critical, rigorous analysis of the topic. However, there are many ways by which the credibility of such information can be compromised.

2. What we think we know but don't really know

This is a common, often serious, problem and comes in many forms, including:

When people who have a superficial knowledge but do not realise that the subject extends far beyond their knowledge. The earlier letter contained an example of a fellow student who came out of an exam proclaiming how easy the exam was, but received a low mark because he did not know that the exam covered material that he did not even know existed.

When *'experts' make decisions in the area of their presumed expertise but err because they are ignorant of something within that area.* [1] The author Malcolm Gladwell illustrated this with an example of an art dealer who approached a major US museum with what he claimed was a marble statue from the sixth century BC. The museum, suspicious that it could be a fake, employed a distinguished geologist to analyse it. The geologist used the whole gamut of sophisticated analytical tools then available and concluded that:

- it was formed from dolomite marble covered by a thin layer of calcite,
- it took aeons for dolomite to change into calcite, and therefore
- the statue was very old — and by implication was genuine.

The museum bought the statue for many millions of dollars. But what the geologist did not know was that dolomite could be changed into calcite in a couple of months using — wait for it — potato mould.

The statue was a fake. The geologist thought he knew what caused dolomite to change into calcite, but he didn't know about the old potato mould trick. I'll return to this statue in the next section.

When decisions are made by groups such as families, committees, councils and other elected bodies and group dynamics and peer pressure amplify the Dunning/Kruger effect (where people who think they know but are mistaken, are strong in asserting their erroneous views), resulting in a decision that has an adverse outcome.

When the evidence, even if correct, does not embrace all the variables affected by the decision. An example from my discipline of veterinary anatomy: a decision was made to decrease the time devoted to dissection because, it was argued, anatomy can be taught equally well by other means including protected specimens, videos and computer simulations.

Support for this decision came from the results of exams, but they tested (only) anatomical knowledge. They did NOT test other attributes that the students were learning, mainly implicitly, during dissection: observing, searching, handling tissues, using surgical/dissection instruments — all of which are important during later, clinical, studies, but of which the decision-makers were ignorant. When dissection was reduced, the students moved into their clinical years deficient in those skills, but they did not know what they were missing. Their clinical teachers noticed that these students were less proficient than their predecessors who had more dissection, but they did not understand why. This was an unintended consequence of the decision on dissection, and it happened because the decision-makers *did not know what they did not know* (and did not bother to find out): that during dissection, students learn much more than could be tested by examinations of 'facts'. Although a specialised example, this illustrates a problem with wider implications.

When the decision-makers have a preconceived view of what the outcome should be. (This can overlap one or more of those mentioned above). In the previous example the real reason may have been related to cost: the videos and specimens could be reused without the recurring cost of dissections.

When the decision-makers have great power but less wisdom or self-awareness. It is not uncommon for politicians to fall into this trap of making decisions based on what they thought they knew, but were wrong.

An example: in 2003 US President George W Bush in 2003 decided to send troops to invade Iraq. He apparently made this decision because he believed they had 'weapons of mass destruction'. But they did not, and there was no convincing evidence that they did or ever had such weapons. Despite that, he used that justification to commit his country to war. More than 250,000 people died.

3. What we know but don't know that (or what) we know.

We are learning all the time, although we may not be aware of it. This implicit (or tacit) learning contributes to memory stores that we cannot describe explicitly, but which we use intuitively in making most decisions.

For example, the students mentioned in the example above were learning skills in observing and in handling instruments and tissues, without being conscious of it. They were building up a bank of *implicit* knowledge in addition to the *explicit* knowledge of anatomic structures that was tested in their exams.

Implicit knowledge is learned more or less unconsciously from experience and experts (including during work experience by students). It is what distinguishes an expert from one who may claim to be expert (and to be able to verbalise tomes of apparently relevant — explicit — information) but lacks the implicit awareness that enables a true expert to solve complex problems.

This was obvious in the saga of the statue described earlier. The geologist provided what he believed was the best available 'evidence' and concluded that the statue must be old and therefore genuine, but a number of art historians expressed concern because they felt that it didn't look right. Within a few seconds, and without being able to articulate the reason, each of them felt — correctly — that the statue was a fraud.

The evidence of the geologist may have been correct, but his interpretation was deficient because he did not know that potato mould could facilitate the rapid conversion of dolomite. But the expert art historians were able to call on their stores of implicit knowledge and immediately identify that the statue was a fraud, even though they may not have been able to explain why.

This phenomenon applies across society. Explicit knowledge may be acquired from factual sources (books, teachers, the internet…), but intrinsic expertise develops from experience, especially if accompanied by constructive feedback. For example an expert cricketer (or tennis player…) will draw on a fund of implicit knowledge when deciding which stroke to play, and an expert racing driver will draw in a fund of implicit knowledge in deciding how to meet the challenges during a race, and so on.

Furthermore, the insights involved in creativity in all fields are dependent to a large — though indeterminate — extent on implicit knowledge, acquired unconsciously and unable to be described explicitly, but which is reflected in innovative solutions, constructions and creations.

Implicit knowledge is of particular importance in the learned professions. In medicine for example, it is what separates the best diagnosticians. They may not be able to explain in detail every part of the process by which they arrive at their diagnostic (or other) decisions, but they are recognised as superior by other doctors with equivalent formal training and experience.

These insights are not new. They have been practiced (if not articulated) by effective teachers for aeons, and were set out more than 40 years ago by pioneer medical educator Hilliard Jason[2]:

> The implications for education appear clear: learning information is important, but far from sufficient. Repetitive practice in the application of information to solution of the same range of problems that will be confronted later is probably mandatory.

4. What we don't know and know that we don't know
If we don't know and want to know, we must consult somebody who does (really) know, and/or search relevant sources, but ensuring that the information gained is: both credible and accurate and precisely relevant to the decision under consideration.

5. What we don't know and don't know that we don't know
This is by far the largest category: prodigious amounts of information exist, but we are completely ignorant of most of it.

Decisions based on computer analysis of big data sets
Decisions that affect us are increasingly being made on the basis of complex mathematical formulae used to interrogate humungous data sets. To a large and increasing extent data, machine learning and predictive analytics drive key decisions that affect our lives. But despite their value in strengthening decision-making, the accuracy, and so the ultimate value, of these analytic tools and algorithms depends on the precision of the knowledge that spawned them[3]. Those who design these instruments are highly expert, but are not immune from the errors that beset individual decision-makers.

Not least it is essential that the data are accurate, are obtained and accessed legally and competently, and are specifically relevant to, restricted to, and embrace the range covered by the decision that results from that analysis.

It would seem that, at least in the USA, transgressions from these and many other logical considerations occur frequently.[4]

In the UK too the problem has become so pervasive that the relevant authority is planning to introduce legally-binding regulations to require firms to explain the basis for algorithms that affect their clients or others[5].

Australia is not immune from similar transgressions. For example, the Federal Court determined that a decision by the government to claim money back from welfare recipients in the Robodebt program was unlawful. The level of debt was being assessed on the basis of one criterion — average income — whereas the size (or even the presence) of such a debt also depends on other criteria[6]. These errors, which resulted from the (mis)use of a decision-making tool by a government ignorant of the scope of that tool, caused immense distress to many welfare recipients.

Implications for education

So often teachers present their (mainly explicit) material by little more than recitation, with few opportunities for their students to develop the implicit skills needed to use that material effectively in decision-making, problem solving, critical thinking or creative endeavours.

Some teachers do provide opportunities to work with the material in tutorials, assignments, practical classes, discussions, or work experience, and some provide constructive feedback. All of these activities can help develop implicit skills, and so provide the learner with the wherewithal to become competent to work with the material in solving problems and making credible decisions. But are they enough?

But do the teachers know how much of those implicit skills their students have acquired? If assessments focus on explicit skills, this is what the students will focus on, and any deficiencies in implicit skills may not become apparent until they are tested in the workplace.

Explanatory notes

1. This example is drawn from the book 'Blink: The Power of thinking without thinking', by Malcolm Gladwell. He had earlier become well known for his observation that a small change, which he termed a tipping point, can often have much larger, unforeseen effects.

2. Relevant aspects of medical decision-making are described in the excellent book 'How Doctors Think' by Jerome Koopman, Professor of Medicine at Harvard University (2008; Houghton, Mifflin). An earlier analysis of medical

decision-making is set out in Medical Problem-solving; an analysis of clinical reasoning, by Arthur Elstein, Lee Shulman and Sarah Sprafka (Harvard University Press, 1978) from Michigan State University, headed by Hilliard Jason. I had the good fortune to be a Fellow in Medical Education there for part of that study.

3. This paragraph was built on insights from data analyst Nick Erzetic.

4. Many problems involving 'big data' are set out in 'Weapons of Math Destruction; how big data increases inequality and threatens democracy' ' by Cathy O'Neill, Penguin Books, 2016.

5. This is explained further in Firms must explain AI decision-making, in New Scientist7 December 2019, p 10.

6. Robodebt. The substance of the error is set out in a judgment made by Justice Davies in The Federal Court of Australia, Victoria Registry on 27 November 2019. Comments on it appear in The Conversation (theconversation.com) on September 17 and 18, October 14 and November 19 and 28, 2019.

Trevor ●◆

Courtesy, respect and the other person...

We interact with other people from the time we are born. Right from the beginning we unconsciously develop our own style as we make various sounds and actions and see what effects they elicit. It is only years later that we are able to think about the effects that we would like to achieve in our interactions with others and make conscious decisions about how to do this.

I'm sure that you have done this a lot already. But there are few points you might like to consider as you deal with the range of personalities that you'll meet as a student, and then in your profession, family and community.

The first is to emphasise the importance of treating all others with courtesy and respect, at least unless and until they show that they are unworthy. Certainly there are some who deserve additional respect — or perhaps it is admiration — for what they have achieved.

That doesn't mean that others are not worthy of respect — and courtesy — as people. Indeed, many young people in the lower echelons of society deserve special recognition — praise or respect — because of what they have done in the circumstances in which they have found themselves.

However my point has a more practical aspect: showing courtesy and respect for one another can make our interactions more effective, and more enjoyable. I well remember one of the leaders of industry in this state stating in a public lecture that 'the most important quality in business is courtesy'.

My second point is that there is much to be gained by viewing inter-personal interactions from the point of view of the other person as well as your own. This involves trying to understand why they are taking that position, what is the history of the issue from their point of view, what pressures are they under, and what they could reasonably expect to gain from the interaction.

Taking these things into consideration doesn't involve being weak or soft, or giving in to unjustifiable demands; in fact it can result in a solution that is more satisfactory to both parties.

Most people have encountered situations where a conflict has escalated so as to cause distress, often to others (such as family members or work colleagues) not party to the original conflict. When confronted by such a situation in my own work, I realised that much of the emotion could be neutralised and acrimony avoided if each party could take a step back and look at the issue from the point of view of the other. It really worked.

An example: as a new Dean I was faced with a senior colleague who was an unsuccessful applicant for my job, and who had transgressed in a major way soon after I started in the job. It could have been seen that he was setting me up, creating an initiation-type test. Other staff were furious and sought sanctions against him. But that would have led to continuing confrontation, and this would be counterproductive. Instead I tried to figure out what might have been behind his action. There was plenty: not only was he disappointed at being passed over for a position he thought was rightfully his, but he had recently to face two family tragedies. While that didn't excuse his behaviour, it did provide an explanation why he behaved in that way at that time. With that in mind, my response was much more measured, and the long-term outcome much more positive: he became one of my strongest supporters.

So this message is simple and two-fold: treat other people with courtesy and respect, and consider potential adversarial situations from the point of view of the other person(s) Ask: what is their background relevant to this issue, how will they interpret those words/actions, and what effect will they have?

I hope you find these points helpful in your interpersonal interactions.

Trevor ●◆

Maintaining relationships...

In previous letters I've written about communication and honesty. These are both critical qualities for a successful relationship, but other factors are also important.

It's a topic I've thought a lot about in the 50+ rewarding years since D and I were married and although I still have much to learn, I thought I'd pass on some things that I have learned about relationships and marriage.

First, our situation: we were married after only a few months courting and it was a small and frugal occasion; we decided to save our few pounds for the future. Back then there was an expectation that wives would stay at home to look after the family, and the laws allowing divorce were centred on adultery. This spawned a sordid business where sleazy men in raincoats and with cameras snooped around bedroom windows hoping to get photographic evidence of infidelity.

Since then the attitudes of society and of lawmakers have become more flexible, and people now feel less constrained by laws and expectations that lacked sense or logic. Women can now contribute to society in a way impossible when we were married: a huge advance. Unfortunately other changes have resulted in less cohesion within families, leading to many marriage breakdowns, often with painful outcomes, especially for kids.

As I contemplated these changes, I started to think about factors that help maintain family unity. It is clear that one of the key factors is mutual trust, respect and concern for each person as they are, rather than how their partner would like them to be. Persistent efforts by one partner to change the other can only lead to protracted disharmony.

Another is for each partner to consider the other when making decisions, small and large, which may affect them both. Thinking, communicating and acting along the lines of: if I did this, what effect would it have on my partner/family; how can I help the other(s) to achieve their aspirations; in other words, adopt an unselfish approach

Then there's love. Important, but what is it, really? How about: intense connectedness of an emotional kind including genuine affection and concern for the other person? The word love is bandied around so much these days, and I sometimes wonder how often declarations of love are based on genuine concern for the other person, and how much on concerns for self. Worth a thought!!

I believe that the factors that I've mentioned - love, mutual trust, concern and respect for the other person — must help maintain the mutual feelings that hold families together. I cannot claim anything like perfection, but I keep trying.

Whatever changes in attitudes to families and relationships occur during your lifetime, I hope you have a stable, rewarding and happy domestic life.

Trevor

Being truthful and honest, and a person of integrity...

The time has come to ask: do you see yourself as a person of integrity? You may ask exactly what do I mean, so I'll explain. I see integrity as a personal code of ethics; a person of integrity is someone who tells the truth and is prepared to face the truth, and is honest and straightforward in all that they do and say. You may hear the term 'a good name' to refer to people of integrity.

You may also be tempted to ask why all people do not follow such a code. The answer is that some are just greedy, concerned for themselves at the expense of others, some are driven by hate or revenge or by the forces of addiction (to drugs, gambling...). Others do so because they convince themselves that the transgression is trivial and that the end justifies the means, and believe that they can get away with it.

That's the sort of thing that prompted this Letter. Some students seek to defer an exam because of inadequate preparation or an inconvenient timetable, and gain the required certification on dubious medical grounds, even telling lies to the certifying doctor.

And — as I mentioned in an earlier Letter, some students use the work of others in assignments or other forms of assessment, and gamble that they can outsmart the anti-plagiarism programs of the institution.

Then there are students who make false claims on their resumes, and justify it because 'everybody does it' or something similar. They may get away with it for a while, but the Internet is replete with examples of senior executives falsifying documents and being caught out — and fired.

These people seem to act as if integrity is an optional extra and who practice honesty, truthfulness and ethical behaviour only when it suits their ends. They think they are smart enough not to get caught. They may get away with dodgy behaviour, but if (or more likely when) they get caught the costs can be calamitous.

They may get away with it for a while, but even if they do not get caught out in a major transgression, many acquire a reputation as being dodgy, untrustworthy, unethical, lacking in integrity. This reputation sticks, and can adversely affect career prospects as well as business and other opportunities, often without the person being aware. They have lost their 'good name' (if they ever had one), and the damage is permanent.

Just a few years ago we learned about the American bankers who devised dodgy deals that earned them squillions, and apparently believed that their minders had built walls high enough to protect them. But those walls did not protect them from major changes in the financial climate. The walls, and the banks, collapsed creating the Global Financial Crisis.

Some, though not enough, of the bankers were forced to change their accommodation from palace to cell, but unfortunately others of the same ilk have since appeared, and are still operating. This became evident recently when a Royal Commission exposed many Australian bankers who were presiding over egregious practices that were adversely affecting their clients, and some were pushed from their gilded pedestals.

University staff are not immune from breaches of integrity. One example (there are many others): a few years ago a local senior academic was caught fabricating 'data' that he had published in an international journal. Incredible!! Obviously he thought he had got away with it, but then a whistle-blower whistled. Now he has gone, his career destroyed.

Many questions. Who would have thought it of him? Why did he cheat, given he had been so successful? Was this the first time? Unlikely: there is evidence that such behaviour often starts early, when transgressors find that they can get away with small transgressions. Such as telling lies to a doctor to gain extra time to prepare for an exam, or making false claims on their resumes.

It seems that apparently small acts of dishonesty are likely to escalate to more serious transgressions especially where the potential reward is high and/or the likelihood of being caught seems low.

It is a slippery slope that is best avoided. I urge you to stay off it.

Trevor ✒

Helping others...

I thought you might be interested to know why I try to help young people facing problems (personal, health, academic, career) and how I go about it.

So firstly, why? I see it as a privilege to be allowed into the lives of other people when they are facing problems, and gain great satisfaction from both helping them to (a) deal with those problems, and (b) develop skills to overcome problems in the future. And I know from my own experience how a small amount of help at a critical point in a young person's life can reap benefit out of all proportion to the time and effort involved

The big question is: how best to go about it? The first step is for the troubled person to ask for, or agree to accept, help. If the troubles are deep-seated and/or serious that step could require a lot of patience and sensitivity. This can be a real problem especially with young men because so many are reluctant to reveal innermost thoughts, even if they know they have a problem.

I've found that troubled young people are most likely to open up if they feel that mutual respect and trust exists between us, that they really matter to me and that I may be prepared to an able to help. It is also important for them to feel that they have my total attention, free from distractions, and that they feel at ease.

This is most likely to be in a neutral location, and without any barriers such as a desk, or negative nonverbal cues such as folded arms or lack of appropriate eye contact. And the whole interaction must be free of any form of real or imagined 'threat', such as a concern that something that they say or do may be used against them. Even then, it can take some time of low-level chat before they feel confident enough to open the door to their problems.

Then comes the question of what to do if the door starts to open. I (try to) remain patient and to listen, observe and be sensitive to the whole message, both the words themselves and the non-verbal cues. This involves keeping an open mind and not jumping to conclusions about what they might say, or prejudging the person or the issue, and letting them finish without interrupting except for any necessary clarification. It also helps to make encouraging noises to indicate that their message is being received.

I also try to see the issues from their point of view, and to try to understand what pressures or other factors are impinging on them. I believe it important to be objective, not judgmental, and to focus on positive points, as well as concentrating on actions, not the person, an to avoid any comments that could be seen as criticism.

Then I would ask 'what can I do to help', and offer constructive, realistic and practical help, including referral to experts if there is any indication that this would help.

A key point: I try to make sure that definite progress is made at that first meeting (and at any others) so that they go away with at least one positive thing that they can do to help ease their problem. I also try hard to follow through and make sure that I do what I say I will do, and also check to see how the issues are progressing for them.

Confidentiality is critical in this whole process. Most young people, especially young men, go to great pains to keep their problems to themselves, and for their friends — and sometimes parents too — not to know. Although it is essential to adhere to their wishes for confidentiality, it is also important that they have the constructive support of friends and, if possible, family.

Although significant other people in their lives may not know the nature of the problems, they may pick up vibes that suggest that something is amiss. In such cases they can bring great comfort by making it clear that they really care.

As I write this I'm reminded of words by American poet Henry Longfellow (1807-1882):

> Give what you have. To someone it may be better than you dare think.

That seems a good point to end this letter. I hope it helps even a little as you seek to help your friends.

Trevor

Looking Forward

Planning for a rewarding, satisfying career...

I've been really impressed that you have taken advantage of your opportunities as a student, but it's now time to consider how best to make the transition to the workplace.

This has interested me for a long time, and I've picked up a few points from surveying graduates and bosses, and much reading and thinking. These points can be combined into one piece of advice: seek to work with the best boss and in the best workplace.

You may ask: what do you mean by best? It means maintaining and encouraging high standards of professional work and ethical behaviour, including impeccable standards of integrity. The best bosses and workplaces also have a good record of:

- encouraging and mentoring graduates;

- treating all people with thoughtfulness and consideration;

- helping staff enhance their knowledge and skills;
- creating conditions where staff look forward to going to work.

You may also ask: why is it so important to start in such a place? Some reasons are obvious, but I'll mention a couple.

1. Standards of work and of ethical behaviour that are established initially are likely to become embedded in the work psyche. If these standards are high, these are likely to be maintained over the years. Conversely, if the standards are low, it is hard to lift them, especially if seeking to move to another position. Furthermore, employers with lower standards are likely to have a reputation that would make it hard for somebody from there to find a job with an employer that seeks to maintain high standards.

2. Initial experiences have a major influence on a graduate's attitudes to that career and their profession generally. I have seen able and eager graduates have their enthusiasm quenched after starting in a toxic or mediocre workplace. Some have seriously questioned their career choice.

Conversely, other graduates who have started with a lukewarm attitude have become highly motivated after starting work with a boss who cares about their people and who maintain high standards of work and integrity.

Trevor

Working with your strengths
and around your weaknesses...

In my last letter I encouraged you to seek the best employer and work-place, especially for your first job. Now I'll encourage you to be a little introspective, and consider your own attributes and how they might apply to your career.

It's natural to think that people will choose a course, and then a career path, in which they can make the most of their strengths (those strong on maths choosing engineering for example).

Unfortunately, this is not always the case, and some choose courses for other reasons, including ease of entry, apparently easy course content, and expectations of earning capacity. This can lead to disappointment and dis-illusionment if jobs do not materialise, or meet expectations or are beyond the ability or personal strengths required.

That's one problem, and it is fairly obvious. One that is less obvious, and which happens too often, is where people with strengths in one area move into a position in another area where personal weaknesses let them down. A good example was a super-smart friend who worked in medical research. Despite his great strengths, he was disappointing and disappointed because he seemed unable to complete and publish his work. Later, apparently on the basis of his superior intellect, he was appointed to head a university department but was a failure there too because he was hopeless as an administrator.

I have seen many other people who have had the value of their strengths neutralised by weaknesses. Some were in a position of financial responsibil-ity but had poor money skills, others had a low tolerance for risk but found themselves in a position of high risk, and others with low tolerance for conflict were in a position of potential conflict.

And, sadly, there are those whose strengths did not include those of integrity and honesty, those with a weakness for gambling or other forms of addiction, and those who become so embroiled in family or other disputes that their work suffers.

Such mismatches between what the job demands and what the person can deliver can lead to considerable stress. In serious cases, it can lead to mental illness, especially clinical depression. Not uncommonly, it seems, the effects of the weaknesses only become evident in retrospect: the position was gained because of the person's strengths, and the weaknesses remained undetected until they lead to some major calamity.

This might all seem a bit hypothetical, so here's an example close to home. A few years ago an engineer with a wide range of great strengths was appointed to progressively senior positions at a local university. It seemed that he had reached the pinnacle of his professional life. But he was forced to resign and was publicly humiliated because of (alleged) breaches of integrity. His case was not an isolated one: similar situations are reported regularly from most careers.

Another example: mine. Like most people in the sciences, I am OK at solving problems — administrative as well as scientific — where the facts and the objectives are fairly clear, but find it stressful when having to work with greater uncertainty. But I found myself in a position where, unexpectedly, I had to work with great uncertainty. This led to a build-up of stress, which, together with a family history of depression, gave succour to the gremlins of depression, and these remain.

What to make of all this? My best thought is that there is merit for each person to try to identify both their weaknesses and their strengths as they apply to their career and to take such steps as they can to avoid situations where the weaknesses can cause problems. Not easy, but worth trying.

I hope that the career path you have chosen is ideally suited to your strengths and that any weaknesses remain in the background.

All the very best for a satisfying, rewarding career.

Trevor

The value of passion, persistence and the pursuit of excellence...

There are a few more points that I should encourage you to think about. The first is to aim to do your best at whatever you do: to achieve excellence.

What does 'excellence' mean to you? To me the meaning given by colleague Dr Ross Fardon has particular appeal. Ross achieved eminence and positions of high leadership in his field of exploration geology but has also thought, read and written widely about the human condition. He describes himself as 'ordinary' and talks with humility but imparts much wisdom and practical common sense. He also stimulates others to think more deeply about what they hope to achieve in their lives. He has certainly had that effect on me, and I thought you might find his thoughts on excellence helpful as you seek to make your way in a changing world.

Ross described excellence as *striving to be better than expected, but not to the level of fanaticism or arrogance,* and observed that it *requires courage and rigour, and achieving a balance between the benefits and the costs and sacrifices involved.*

He is convincing in his assertion that *excellence in practice is vision + creativity + balance + clarity + process. A large part of the vision must be all the human virtues, starting with respect and honesty.*

As I thought about that definition, I realised the importance of the word 'striving' — striving to be better — and that this flows from being passionate — enthusiastic, excited, dedicated, committed — about what we're doing; being persistent in pursuing our passion.

This line of thought led to the conclusion that passion can be a key contributor to success in a career. Those who feel passionate about what they are doing are more likely to put in extra effort, to see and take opportunities that are invisible to others less passionate, and most importantly, to see the work as worthwhile and enjoyable.

Of course, passion is only one component, albeit a valuable one, of a successful career. That also requires mastery of relevant explicit and implicit knowledge and skills coupled with the ability to use these to complete required tasks in an acceptable way.

In almost all cases, achieving 'success' also involves the ability to relate effectively to other people, whether clients or patients, colleagues at other levels in a hierarchy, or members of the community generally.

As I cogitated on these points, it became evident that passion could be the guiding light to focus on as circumstances and opportunities change over your career.

It is generally agreed that many current jobs will disappear as technology advances and that most people will need to change career directions periodically. Even with relevant higher-order cognitive, affective and communication skills, it may be hard to see a way forward, both financially and with a feeling that what they are doing is worthwhile.

If you are in this position you may find it helpful to ask yourself: what is my (real) passion? Is it, for example, to make heaps of money, or to help other people, or to influence other people, or to save the planet...?

And then in relation to a potential career direction, to ask: is this consistent with my passion? I realise that you'll need to take into account many other factors — what is available, what is consistent with your personality, abilities, responsibilities and susceptibilities — but hope that it can help to navigate through the shifting quicksands in the job market and maintain a satisfying and rewarding working and personal life.

Another point: you may find that your passion can only be fulfilled as secondary to the main position. My passion has always been to help young people achieve their objectives, but have found that opportunities to do this were often diluted by having to deal with a plethora of distracting tasks. But I persisted despite these distractions, and felt that I gained much more than I gave; such is the power of passion.

I'll finish with the hope that you will find a niche (or a succession of them) in which you can fulfil your passion and achieve excellence, while also living a balanced, rewarding life. I will be happy to do whatever I can to help bring that about.

Trevor

What does 'profession' mean to you?...

Now that you are planning to join a profession — to become a professional (person) — I'd like to encourage you to think about what these terms mean.

It's something I've thought a lot about over the years, and I'll pass on what I've discovered.

First thing I figured out was that the use of the term in the oldest profession is not relevant or helpful, so will not mention it again.

The current usage probably developed from the term 'learned profession' which was used a couple of hundred years ago to refer to law, medicine and religion. Now the 'learned' bit has been dropped from the name, although a high level of learning, both initially and for the longer term, is still essential.

So is the need to maintain high standards of integrity and ethical behaviour, and to act in the best interests of clients or patients, without self-interest.

Members of most professions are now regulated by law and overseen by regulatory bodies, and these act to maintain standards of technical and ethical performance and behaviour, and to punish those who transgress.

It is important though to realise that these regulatory bodies — such as The Australian Medial Council — are separate from the professional associations — The Australian Medical Association — which advocate for their members and provide services including continuing education.

So what is a profession? One of Australia's best-respected lawyers (and Chancellor of the University of NSW), David Gonski, when addressing a medical audience, took these points further and gave the most perceptive description of a profession that I have seen: He said that it involves:

> First, a willingness to help younger members learn and achieve. Second, a thirst to keep abreast of the latest techniques, writing and knowledge

of the discipline. Third, a commitment to working with your patients (or, in my case, clients) assisting them in an ethical and beneficial way, without any conflict of interest. Fourth, a desire to give back, both to the profession and to the community. Finally, and really arising from the previous four, a pride in what the profession does and what you do in its name.

This was published in his book *I gave a Gonski. Selected speeches by David Gonski*, published by Penguin Books in 2015, and I commend this to you.

I have great confidence that you can do all this and look forward to watching your progress towards becoming a highly respected member of your profession. I will do whatever I can to help bring that about.

Trevor

Convincing the best employer...

I was so pleased that you have decided where you would like to start your career. Now comes the interesting part: convincing an employer that you are the person for their position.

At the start, I believe that it is useful to place yourself in the position of the employer and ask: what attributes do I have that will they see as valuable, and how should I present these in the best possible light? You will then set these out in a resume (or curriculum vitae or cv), and send it off either online and/or with a letter of transmission in the hope of being selected for the next stage, usually an interview, sometimes with testing or other hurdles.

These documents should reflect you as a person, and so I will not be too prescriptive about how you should construct yours. Instead, and in keeping with my objective of helping you develop your own skills, I will set down some of the principles that I believe to be important and let you use them as you see fit.

The resume. This should be a clear, concise, and honest personal account of your attributes relevant to the position, presented in a logical and professional way. Start with name and contact details, and a short summary statement, then:

- Concentrate on the positions, awards or grades that are recent, relevant or significant.

- Be arranged so that the (most recent) key points, are in a prominent position.

- Reflect your personal style. I remember an employer observing that he knew which applicants had been to my talk on getting jobs; their resumes all looked the same.

- Draw attention to things that you have done that indicate your suitability for that position. Examples (and there could be many others) include:

  - being in a winning crew/team should indicate self-discipline, and persistence;

  - working in a pub, or servo should indicate the ability to work with clients;

  - being elected to an office indicates acceptance for a leadership role... and so on.

- Provide a list, usually three, of referees. I suggest asking (and always ask before nominating them) people who know you well, are likely to say good things about you, and are likely to be regarded by the employer as credible.

I also believe that the resume should NOT:

- be an uncritical recitation of accomplishments;

- contain abbreviations, acronyms or other terms that may not be known to a reader;

- contain any partial or complete untruths. As mentioned in my letter about integrity, some people do try this, and many are caught.

If *a letter of transmission* is needed, remember that this will usually be read first, so that it should entice the reader to read on — to the resume.

It should be presented in an impeccably professional way, addressed to a person, never to an anonymous Sir/Madam or To Whom it May Concern.

Most such letters consist of three main parts:

1. A sentence stating its purpose: Please accept this letter and the attached resume as an application for the position of....

2. An account of attributes that make you stand out for that position, presented in a persuasive style and not simply as a précis of the resume;

3. A final statement: I would be most grateful for the opportunity to discuss my application, and can make myself available at your convenience...I suggest that you draft the letter, put it aside for a day

or two, then review it, asking 'is this word/sentence necessary, or could it be deleted or reworked to make the meaning more succinct and clearer, and check for any errors of spelling or syntax.

It is also worth seeking feedback from someone with experience in evaluating job applications.

If you are invited for an interview, find out as much as you can about the enterprise so that you can discuss it intelligently. And remember that you will be being judged as a young professional in that workplace, so dress, speak and behave accordingly, and bear in mind that a key criterion for selection is an agreeable personality.

I hope that you will be successful in your application to the 'best' employer and that this will lead to a rewarding, productive and enjoyable career.

Starting work...

Congratulations on getting that job. I was especially pleased for you that you could start your career in a field you are passionate about, and in an environment where you will be mentored and learn, be cared about, and where you will enjoy working.

You'll probably be feeling a bit nervous about starting, so I'll pass on a few tips that I've learned from recent graduates and their employers. Most are pretty obvious, but my spies tell me that some graduates need a few reminders. So here goes:

- *Make an effort to fit in from the beginning.* That's obvious; you will want to be comfortable working there. But there are some practical reasons too: if you behave in a courteous, thoughtful and friendly way (which I'm sure you would anyway), colleagues will be more likely to support, help and 'protect' you, especially when you are still feeling a bit lost. Fitting in also extends to grooming and other personal habits (and body odour was mentioned in my surveys), and that you do not leave rubbish around for others to clean up. May seem trivial, but really important.

- *See yourself as a professional person,* and dress, speak and behave accordingly. Some graduates, after years of dressing, speaking and acting in student mode, do need to pay enough attention to this, especially initially. But I think you will find that if you do make an effort to see yourself in professional work mode, it will be much easier to adopt that mode in your thinking and working.

- *Make it clear that you are keen to learn.* Watch and listen, pay attention to any induction activities, read and absorb any relevant information — and think. If, having thought you are still unsure, then ask questions. I hear that some graduates have trouble getting the right balance between asking too little (which may be interpreted as lack of either interest or willingness to learn), or asking too much, especially before thinking and trying to work out the answer. Concentrating on thinking before asking can help get the balance right.

- *Stay fit in body and mind.* As you will find, starting in a new job can be tiring and at times stressful. Exercise is a great way to dissipate stress, and joining a sporting club is also a great way to make new friends. This is especially important for those who have to shift to a new location to take up the job.

I've found that those who maintain contact with friends are less likely to suffer adverse effects from stress. Some relieve this by regaling their peers with war stories … 'you should have heard what happened to me' …being countered by 'that's nothing compared to what happened to ME!' Nowadays there are many ways to stay in contact, but, surprisingly, many graduates do not take advantage of them.

With every good wish for a wonderful future.

Trevor

Looking forward to an uncertain future...

I was pleased to hear you have settled well into your new job, and that your boss and work environment are stimulating, congenial and supportive. I know that you'll do your best so that you will be in a good position to move forward in your career.

I know that it would be easy to become concerned about predictions of major job losses as more tasks are taken over by technology. But creating and working with the new technology will also open up new opportunities, many of which we cannot predict.

I encourage you to prepare yourself to take advantage of new situations as they emerge. How to do that? I have previously opined that you will enhance your chances by:

- *working* with bosses and in workplaces that maintain the highest professional, interpersonal and ethical standards, and doing your best at whatever you do;

- *developing* higher-level cognitive (as in problem-solving, creativity, ingenuity), affective (aka emotional intelligence) and communication skills, coupled with an overarching passion, will help you to navigate the changing landscape of the future.

Specifically, I suggest you pay particular attention to:

- *Critical thinking*: a bit of a cliché I know, but to me, it means the ability to separate fact from opinion, to reflect, question, and to reason clearly, logically, rigorously and without bias.

  Furthermore, when making or evaluating decisions, adopt a sceptical approach to relevant evidence: is it relevant, credible, rigorous, covering the focus of the decision and no more, or is it biased, corrupt(ed) or otherwise unreliable?

These qualities will increasingly be necessary, not only to retain an objective focus but also to avoid making unwise moves in the maze of start-ups, break-outs and other entrepreneurial ventures that may tempt you.

- *Commitment* to building up your knowledge and skills that can be applied in new and creative ways.

- *Self-awareness and the willingness to be self-critical:* to analyse your own behaviour and performance in a rigorous way, and to take corrective action.

- *Ethical behaviour,* which could become a minefield when advances — as in increasing the length of life (either and the beginning or the end) — creates ethical dilemmas.

- *Cultural competence,* the ability to move freely between countries and cultures as borders become increasingly irrelevant.

Although all workplaces will change — and in ways as yet unknown – the likelihood of taking advantage of those changes is likely to increase if a conscious effort is made to identify fundamental strengths (including passions) and weaknesses. These may include (but are not restricted to):

- low tolerance for uncertainty and ambiguity;

- inability to plan or to consider broader issues;

- inability to see the importance of precise, accurate detail;

- regarding integrity and honesty as optional extras, and

- functional illiteracy with numbers and/or finances

They can be disastrous for somebody who unwittingly strays into a position requiring these skills. While some weaknesses can be overcome by training, others are so deep-seated that they can lead to major career problems and/or serious mental illness.

Strengths, which for many are the basis of passions, will be most likely to bring fulfilment if in a position where the strength is valued/rewarded. If such a position is not available initially, do not despair, but take all reasonable steps to demonstrate what you are capable of doing to contacts within and without that workplace. The value of your strengths will increase to the extent that you are able to become engaged/immersed in the tasks.

Getting the best job: seek a workplace, especially a first one, which has a:

- boss who maintains high standards of ethics, professional work and constructive concern for staff;

- record for encouraging, training and mentoring staff (especially recent graduates), and for concern for their welfare and future. NB: current staff are often a valuable source of this information.

But do not worry too much if you cannot identify a specific area of strength/passion. I've found that many such people have a range of aptitudes and that one or more of these will flourish if they work under a 'good' (=able, stimulating, concerned) boss in a congenial workplace, to the best of their ability, and show a willingness to accept constructive feedback, and to learn.

I hope you will find that whatever direction the future takes you it will bring much satisfaction, reward, health and happiness.

Trevor ✒

Distilling the Essence

The future...

As I think back over all those letters, I'm left with the feeling that I've given you a lot to digest, and that there might be merit in trying to distil out — even to repeat — the key ingredients. So here goes:

Learning
Learning information (explicit learning) occurs most effectively if based on principles already learned; learning how to use that information usually occurs unconsciously (as implicit learning) and involves relevant practice preferably with constructive feedback. This may or may not be provided during university courses.

Knowing
Is not a clearcut concept: we know much more than we are conscious of knowing, and we may think we know something but are fooling ourselves. Not uncommonly people who think that they know something but are mistaken are also vehement in promulgating their erroneous beliefs. This, the Dunning-Kruger effect, can underlie bad decisions, especially by groups.

Heads

Decreased enthusiasm, energy, engagement, motivation or other changes in behaviour point to a need for:

- expert medical attention, initially a GP with special interest and training in mental health (not shared by all GPs);

- credible online support such as beyondblue.org.au;

- nonjudgmental and constructive personal support;

- encouragement to engage in appropriate exercise and appropriate engaging activity (music, nature, a project).

Interacting

Communicating: sending a message from your brain to the brain of another person. The likelihood of it being received clearly and unambiguously should increase if care is taken with each stage of the process, including:

- the sender of the message selecting appropriate:

    - words; both meaning and emotional flavour;
    - means of transmission: in person, phone, SMS…

- nonverbal cues, some of which (e.g. facial expressions and body movements) may be selected unconsciously, but others such as dress (casual or formal, indicative of position such as white coat), or location (their place or yours or neutral) have a conscious component.

- the receiver listening actively, not interrupting or prejudging.

Relationships, the workplace and life generally, have a higher chance of a being effective if:

- based on courtesy and mutual respect,

- each trusts the other, believing that they will act with integrity (remembering that a single act of dishonesty can destroy trust).

- both sides try to see the issue from other person's point of view, trying to understand what led to the current situation.

Deciding

When making or evaluating decisions, adopt a sceptical approach to relevant evidence: is it relevant, credible, rigorous, covering focus of decision and no more, or is it biased, corrupt(ed) or otherwise unreliable?

Working

Although all workplaces will change — and in ways as yet unknown — the likelihood of taking advantage of those changes is likely to increase if a conscious effort is made to identify fundamental strengths (including passions) and weaknesses.

Weaknesses can be disastrous for somebody who unwittingly strays into a position requiring these skills. While some weaknesses can be overcome by training, others are so deep-seated that they can lead to major career problems and/or serious mental illness.

Strengths, which may be the basis of passions, will be most likely to bring fulfilment if in a position where the strength is valued/rewarded.

Getting the best job: seek a workplace which has a:

- boss who maintains high standards of ethics, professional work and constructive concern for staff;

- record for encouraging, training and mentoring staff (especially recent graduates), and for concern for their welfare and future.

Do not worry if you cannot immediately identify a specific area of strength/passion. I've found that many such people have a range of aptitudes, and that one or more of these will flourish if they work under a 'good' (= able, stimulating, concerned) boss in a congenial workplace, to the best of their ability, and show a willingness to accept constructive feedback, and to learn.

The future

I believe that those most likely to flourish as conditions change will:

- do their best at whatever they do;

- be in command of the basic principles of their disciplines;

- be adept at solving higher-level problems and at being creative;

- demonstrate a commitment to continue to learn and to be flexible;

- be able to communicate effectively to a variety of audiences, and

- do their best to be seen as indispensable in whatever they do.

I hope you will find that whatever direction the future takes you it will bring much satisfaction, reward, health and happiness.

Trevor